MONEY BOOK NO. 7

HOW TO SAVE ON TAXES

And Take All the Deductions You Are Entitled To

Published by

George Sterne
Profit Ideas
8361 Vickers St., Suite 304
San Diego, CA 92111

Printed in Mexico

The Money Books

1. Plant your dollars in Real Estate and Watch them Grow
2. How to make money in the Stock Market
3. Secrets of the Millionaires - How the Rich Made it Big
4. The Pocket Book of Personal Money Management
5. Secrets of Banking and Borrowing
6. How to Start Making Money in a Business of your own
7. How to Save on Taxes - and take all the deductions you're entitled to.

Copyright © 1980 George Sterne
Library of Congress catalog card number 78-64393

How to Save on Taxes --
And Take all The Deductions You Are Entitled To

TABLE OF CONTENTS

FORWARD

FORWARD

This book is designed to help you weather the whimsical storms of Congressional folly. A game plan against the IRS campaign to separate you from your money is badly needed at a time when government consumes 48 cents out of every dollar earned by the average American taxpayer.

Spiced with a twist of humor and peppered with a healthy moral philosophy in defiant opposition to the parasitical and debillitating nature of taxation, this book is both a practical guide and an inspirational enlightenment. It is as much meat and potatoes as it is tonic and ginger. Not only does it lay out a set of tax-saving strategies for you to follow, but it is enlivened with a clear message of moral responsibility. Not a responsibility to pay taxes, but a responsibility to the principles of freedom and individual rights. Make no mistake about it, taxation is legally sanctioned theft. It is the manifestation of government fiat and political force. You have a responsibility to yourself, to your family, and to the cause of liberty to do whatever is necessary to hand over as little as you have to to the bandits going under the euphemistic heading of "Internal Revenue Service."

The first section of this "tax trilogy" encompasses much fascinating subject material. It can be used as subject matter for lively speeches, as entertaining facts for party conversation, or as motivational fuel for building the courage that is necessary to challenge the IRS. The second section delves into the basics. The last section explores dynamic strategy options.

Cold numerical tax facts, legal information, and strategic maneuvers are brought to life in this book. Matter is interlaced with spirit, strategy is fused with philosophy, and facts are salted with wit and humor.

PART ONE

THE TAX DRAIN

"Now to rob one's friendly neighbor
  May indeed be very wrong;
Unless, of course, in doing it
  the voters go along!
This makes it quite respectable,
  as all of course agree;
For isn't this the meaning of Democracy?

Richard Grant

Chapter One

TAXES, TAXES EVERYWHERE, AND NOT
AN END IN SIGHT ......

"There is one difference between a tax collector and a taxidermist; the taxidermist leaves the hide."

Mortimer Caplin
Former Director of the IRS

Nothing is more true than the well-known and oft repeated assertion that there are only two sure things is this world: death and taxes.

Over 150 hidden taxes are included in the price of a single loaf of bread. There are 116 indirect taxes levied on a suit of clothes and 100 such taxes surreptitiously attached to a carton of eggs.

Federal, state, regional and municipal taxes are to blame. There are federal, state and city income taxes — both corporate and personal. We pay property taxes, excise taxes, sales taxes, inventory taxes, special district taxes, estate taxes, intangibles taxes, capital gains taxes, payroll taxes, franchise taxes, gift taxes and unemployment insurance taxes. Then there is Social Security as well as license fees, fines and permits.

While it only costs ten cents to produce *one barrel* of Arabian crude oil (that's less than a quarter cent per gallon), we pay nearly a dollar a gallon at the pump. Most of the price increase comes from taxes.

The Arabian government oil cartel (OPEC) tacks on a stiff royalty tax which accounts for the biggest chunk of the high price for gas. The United States government then slaps a tariff on imported oil. The refiners, processors and distributors pay a long list of federal, state and local taxes. The gas station operator has to charge the consumer to pay for these taxes as well as the excise tax and sales tax the service station has to pay.

A gallon of gas is priced at 420 times higher than the original drilling cost. Most of this is due to taxes.

To stay in business, every firm must *at least* break even. The businessman must cover his costs. When costs increase, the businessman has no choice but to raise prices. Since taxes are a major cost of doing business, it should come as no surprise to anyone that every tax which is assessed on a business is passed down to the consumer of the company's products.

The consumer ultimately pays the employees' withholding taxes. The income tax shouldered by the corporations and the estimated tax born by self-employed entrepreneurs is really paid for by the consumer.

In addition to gasoline, special excise taxes are levied on alcohol, tobacco, motor vehicles and automobile parts.

Taxes may be defined as the legislative demand for

mandatory exaction of money from an otherwise unwilling person. Taxation is mandatory, not voluntary.

The innumerable regulatory costs that have been thrown on business by government are one such involuntary expense. Regulation is a form of taxation. The costs of complying with the endless array of senseless statutes are unnecessary production costs which have been legislated on business by government. The indirect tax, called regulation — like any other tax — is passed on to the consumer.

Whenever government spends more than it takes in, it incurs a deficit. Deficits are covered by printing dollars (the government calls this "monetizing the debt"). What this means is that they are inflating the money supply.

When more dollars are chasing fewer goods, prices rise. Inflation is a cost which is involuntarily inflicted on the American citizenry. Inflation, like regulation, is yet another example of a devastating hidden tax.

Ultimately, the consumer foots the bill for every single tax government forces us to pay. *Everyone* is a consumer. We are *all* hurt by excessive taxes.

A wide spectrum of taxes − of just about every sort and variety imaginable − has foisted higher prices on the American consumer. The price tag on every automobile, comb and jelly bean includes a long string of buried taxes and *no one* can escape paying them.

The cost of the gas you burn in your car is mostly tax.

You must pay registration and license fees. You may have to pay a toll to get on a state thoroughfare. When your car isn't running, there are parking fees, parking meters, meter maids and tickets.

The government taxes the interest you earn from your savings account, the dividends you receive from stocks and the income you make from a wage, salary or capital gain. You pay taxes every time you turn on a light, pick up the phone and turn up the heater or air conditioner.

You pay taxes every time you pour yourself a drink, light up a cigarette or turn on the stove; every time you take in a play, go to a movie or go out to dinner.

A good part of the mortgage or rent is ear-marked for taxes. You pay taxes when you buy a diamond, sell a diamond or keep a diamond. You pay taxes whenever you fly on an airplane, travel by train or cruise on a ship.

You pay taxes when you earn money, when you save it and when you spend it. You pay taxes if you give someone a generous gift.

They'll get you when you work, when you play, when you drive, fly or ski. They will tax your home, your investments, your clothes, your family heirlooms, your property, your working time and the things you eat.

To repeat once again, there are federal, state and city, personal and corporate income taxes. There are personal and commercial, state, county and municipal property taxes. There are assessments on people living within special districts and there are forced exactions levied by regional governmental entities. There are excise taxes on gasoline, alcohol, tobacco, motor vehicles and automobile parts.

There are sales taxes, inventory taxes, estate taxes, intangibles taxes, capital gains taxes, payroll withholding taxes, franchise taxes, gift taxes, unemployment insurance taxes, value-added taxes, social security taxes, license fees, fines, permits, tariffs, regulatory costs, inflation . . . .

Taxation has reached such unbearable proportions in countries like Sweden that is now possible to pay a 102 percent income tax. Actor Ingmar Bergman was broadsided with a 139 percent tax assessment before leaving his native Sweden.

In America, *a double* tax has been dumped on dividend income. The government taxes corporate income before it is distributed to the stockholders as dividends, where it is taxed again. If the stockholder is unfortunate enough to have earned $200,000 a year or more, and if the corporation earns more than $50,000, the hopeless taxpayer is hit for a combined 84 percent tax!

If the corporation was lucky enough to be operating on a six percent profit margin, the stockholder is getting *less than a one percent return* on his money. With less than one percent, he can't even keep up with inflation.

In 1964, an iconoclastic rock group burst the traditional

seams which had stitched together American culture, values and music. A few meteoric years later, in the wake of dazzling financial success, the Beatles became frustrated with the prohibitive tax structure in the British welfare state. The group's disillusionment with high taxes was reflected in the song "Tax Man", where the musicians refrained, "If you drive your car, I'll tax the street; if you try to walk, I'll tax your feet".

Americans believe that they have a responsibility to support their government, but not in the style to which it has become accustomed.

"At the same time, heavier public burdens have further restricted his freedom by lessening that portion of his earnings which he can spend as he pleases and augmenting the portion taken from him to be spent as public agents please."

Herbert Spender

CHAPTER TWO

TAX FACTS

"What is wanted is a wise and frugal government which shall not take from the mouth of labor the bread it has earned."

Thomas Jefferson

Thirty-seven cents out of every dollar earned in 1978 was siphoned off in direct taxes to government. *Indirect* taxes siphoned off another eleven cents.

WHAT THIS MEANS IS THAT GOVERNMENT SHAVES 48 CENTS OFF EVERY DOLLAR THAT IS EARNED.

One out of every five people works for the government. One out of every five dollars spent on goods and services is paid for by government. Government outlays consume 41 percent of the national income. One dollar out of every $3.80 in personal income is met by direct government payments.

A crushing 482 billion dollar burden was delivered to the American taxpayer in 1976 — 14 percent more than was chiselled away in 1975. The pelting was 146 percent larger than the 196 billion dollars whisked away in 1966.

Direct taxes only took ten cents out of every dollar in 1929. They chipped off 26 cents in 1946. Government was pinching off 30 cents by 1956. They squeezed out 32 cents in 1966; they scratched away 36 cents in 1976. Today, they seize 37 cents out of every dollar the average American earns. And when the indirect taxes are considered as well, the average American is bitten by a 48 percent tax shakedown.

What this means, in concrete terms, is that 48 percent of the average American's working life is spent working for the government. The average American taxpayer works from January first until May sixteenth, just to pay the *direct* taxes to government. That's the same as working two hours and forty-eight minutes out of every eight hour work day.

When *both* the direct and the indirect taxes are included, the average taxpayer has to work for the government from January first until June twenty-fifth. *On June twenty-sixth, we get to start working for ourselves.* Government clips off three hours and fifty minutes out of every eight hour working day.

For the person on a nine-to-five job, it might be of some comfort to know that the money you earn after 12:50 is yours to keep!

The serfs in the dark ages used to toil three months of the year for the feudal lord. Because of this unbearably oppressive 25 percent "tax rate", they frequently tried escaping through the swamps.

In comparison to the 48 percent (or six months) tax toil endured by the modern taxpayer, the liability thrust upon the medieval serf looks mild. It should become immediately apparent that a great part of our lives is spent in servitude. We are 48 percent slave and 52 percent free men.

The story is even worse for people in high income brackets. Because of the highly graduated, and deeply punitive income tax, it comes as no surprise that IRS figures show the more prosperous half of the population shouldering 93 percent of the tax burden.

The upper 25 percent (anyone earning $15,898 or more per year) carries 75 percent of the load. The upper ten percent (anyone earning more than $23,420) picks up nearly half the tab.

There were only 1,149 people who earned more than a million dollars in 1975. The average individual in this bracket was taken for a $1,011,317 ride.

Over half the income returns (56.8 percent) are filed by people who earn less than $10,000; yet only 12.8 percent of the total tax "revenue" collected by government comes from people in this income bracket. Those people who are earning less than $10,000 a year account for much less than their fair pro rata share. Their proportionate burden is only 20 percent of the otherwise equally distributed per capita load!

While filed IRS returns show that 18.8 percent of the people earn between ten and fifteen thousand dollars, only 17.4 percent of the taxes collected by the federal government come from that group. Their pro rata share of the tax burden is just 90 percent of the per capita amount.

It's not until the taxpayer starts earning $17,000 or more that he starts paying more than his per capita share of taxes.

Twelve percent of the people earn between fifteen and twenty thousand dollars, and that same 12 percent accounts for 17.8 percent of the taxes paid to government. They shoulder a pro rata burden that is one and a half times the per capita share.

Only 8.7 percent of the people earn between twenty and thirty thousand dollars, yet 20.7 percent of the taxes bilked from the American taxpayer come from the members of this income bracket. Their pro rata share is 2.4 times the per capita level.

The individual earning $29,000 a year is carrying a pro rata load which is *three times the size* of the per capita level.

Those who earn between thirty and fifty thousand dollars make up just 2.6 percent of the population, yet they account for 12.3 percent of the taxes. Their pro rate share is 4.7 times the per capita load.

While only 9/10 of one percent of the people earn between fifty and one hundred thousand dollars, they come up with 12.3 percent of the taxes - for an unwieldy pro rata share of 10.9 times the per capita level.

A mere 2/10 of one percent of the people make more than $100,000. Yet people in that group are butchered for 8.3 percent of the taxes, to carry a staggering pro rate share of 41.5 times the per capita burden!

In spite of the never-ending stream of drivel forever gushing out of the mouths of populist demagogues, people in the upper income brackets most certainly pay their taxes. And if the politicians would only put their brains in gear before putting their mouths in motion, they would realize that *the only social injustice going on is that the most prosperous, the most productive members of our society are paying far far more than their fair share of taxes.*

In 1970, only 112 out of the 15,323 people who earned more than $200,000 were able to slip through the IRS dragnet. Less than 3/4 of one percent escaped paying federal income tax.

Only 153 such lucky people wiggled out of the clutches of the IRS in 1973. A lucky band of 244 citizens successfully climbed through the 1974 obstacle course of deductions, credits and tax shelters to avoid paying income tax.

Out of the 34,121 people who earned more than $200,000 in 1975, only 230 paid no federal income tax. Once again, less than ¾ of one percent successfully meandered through that maze of tax laws, rubber stamps and red tape. *The remaining 99.7 percent handed over 63 percent of their income to the Internal Revenue Service.*

It is no wonder why the word "budget" comes from the French word "bougette" which means a small bag. Because *that* is what the taxpayer is left holding.

Your income must grow by 35 percent each year just to stay ahead of taxes and inflation.

When the social security tax was first instituted in 1937, only $3,000 of a person's wages could be taxed in the name of "social security". And the combined tax rate was just two percent — one percent from the employee and one percent from the employer.

In 1950, the combined rate assessed both employer and employee was increased to three percent. Then, in 1951, the members of Congress lifted the maximum wage that could be taxed (the "wage base") from $3,000 to $3,600. The combined tax rate was boosted to four percent in 1954 and the "wage base" dilated to $4,200 in 1955.

Once again, Congress raised the tax rate to four and a half percent in 1957. They jacked up the tax rate to five percent *and* increased the "wage base" to $4,800 in 1959. The tax rate was hoisted to six percent in 1960.

In 1962, they inflated the tax rate to 6.3 percent. The tax rate grew to 7.3 percent in 1963. Just three years later the rate climbed to 7.7 percent and the "wage base" swelled to $6,600.

The social security tax rate was beefed up to 7.8 percent in 1967. The "wage base" ballooned to $7,800 and the tax

13

rate jumped to 8.8 percent in 1968.

The government pushed up the tax rate to 9.6 percent in 1969. They bumped up the rate to 10.4 percent in 1971. They enlarged it to 11.3 percent in 1973. It stood at 11.7 percent in 1977.

The present round of social security tax hikes — starting in 1978 and ending in 1987 — *will bloat the taxable "wage base" to $31,200 and magnify the social security tax to 12.9 percent.*

The maximum social security tax will *triple* in just ten years — from 1978's $1,930 to 1987's $6,092. The maximum social security tax will have multiplied *more than one hundred times* since its inception in 1937.

Social security snatched 25 billion dollars in 1966 — and lopped off 84 billion dollars in 1976.

Social security is a geometrically propagating financial chain letter. Those who are reaping today's social security benefits are committing working youths to a sinking retirement program that, in years to come, will be no more solvent than the Penn Central Railroad or the Post Office. The young people who are forced to contribute to social security today will not benefit from the program when they reach retirement age — because the system will be broke.

But let's suppose, for the sake of argument, that the system *doesn't* go broke. Let's assume that social security will, in fact, meet the obligations it has committed itself

14

to. If this could happen, does it mean the recipient of social security can come out ahead?

No.

Take the case of a laborer pulling down $16,000 a year. He pays $936 a year for social security. His employer matches it with another $936. A total of $1,872 is applied toward his social "security" retirement plan each year.

The laborer works 37 years and sinks $69,264 into social security (the average man works about 37 years). At retirement age, the average worker has 101 months left to live. He will draw $589.60 a month from social "security". He will get back an expected total of $59,549.60 — almost $10,000 *less than he put into it.*

If the worker had been allowed to save his money in a private bank and earn just a meager *five percent interest,* the $69,264 deposited over 37 years would have waxed to a $195,000 sum — enough to retire on a monthly pension of $812.50.

Not only would the worker get a pension that was more than the amount he could ever hope to get from social security, but he would also have a tidy inheritance he could pass on to his children. In addition to getting a nicer pension from his private plan, the worker could leave to his heirs a sum of money substantially *larger than the total sum he could get from social security.*

The prime example of the excessive surge of oppressive taxes is, of course, the federal income tax.

The first income tax was drafted as an emergency measure to subsidize the fighting of the civil war. It was repealed in 1872.

Congress tried to re-institute the income tax in 1894, by slipping it in as a seemingly innocuous rider to a tariff bill. It night-sticked anyone earning more than $4,000 a year and made the people fork over two percent of their hard-earned money to the bureaucrats, politicians and tax collectors in Washington.

The Supreme Court declared the income tax unconstitutional in 1895. The total amount collected that year was just $77,000! Since a tax on land was a direct tax, any tax on income from land was also a direct tax. And direct taxes, as stated in Article I, Section 2, Clause 3 of the Constitution may not be assessed unless apportioned in direct relationship to the population of every state.

This legal setback discouraged the politicians for the short order of 14 years. President Taft, in 1909, launched an effort to hurdle the unconstitutional obstacle posed by the income tax by advocating the passage of a constitutional amendment. Few people thought Taft had any chance of getting the required 36 states to ratify the amendment. To make the pill less bitter to swallow, Taft proposed a $3,000 personal deduction and a lean one percent tax on anyone earning less than $20,000. His idea of a "graduated" tax was neither overly harsh nor excessively gruelling (by today's standards). The hardest the income tax could hit anyone was 7 percent; and it only nicked people who earned more than $500,000.

Taft let it be known the government would allow several deductions to be made against income. The people were taken in by the side-show of political mountebanks. A public sigh of relief went up knowing that interest paid on personal debts, local tax payments, business expenses and losses, depreciation, bad debts and the losses from fire, storm or shipwreck wouldn't be taxed. It was a little like thanking the inquisitor for chopping off your finger instead of your arm.

Taft's proposed amendment sailed through Congress and was sent to the states for ratification. Alabama wins the dubious prize for taking just thirty days to be the first state to ratify what was to become the 16th Amendment. Cheek to jowl, the rest of the states were duped into casting their approval of the income tax amendment. It became official law in February of 1913 — when Massachussetts (who wins second prize) became the thirty-sixth state to ratify.

The first 1040 form was four pages only — including instructions. The printing was in big letters, and there was lots of empty space. There were no schedules A, B, C . . . . . .

At no time in history have so many people been hood-winked into believing a tax would never become burdensome. After all, the government saddled the 1916 citizenry with a combined 68 million dollars in income taxes. They were paying more in tobacco excise taxes (88 million dollars) and alcohol excise taxes (247 million dollars).

More than three and a half times as much money was milked out of the public for alcohol excise taxes than for income taxes. "The income tax", pontificated the government, "is not something to get very excited over".

Sure enough, when the government hiked the maximum income tax from 7 to 15 percent in 1916, and the taxes purloined from the upper-most income bracket escalated, few people got very excited. "After all", reasoned the average citizen, "they are just pronging the rich, and the rich need a good soaking".

And likewise, very few people complained when the politicians began their sleight-of-hand tricks and levitated the maximum tax rate to 24 percent in 1929. The government inched up the tax to 25 percent in 1930. The politicians log rolled, back scratched, coughed and voted in 1935 to send the rate bolting skyward to 63 percent. By 1941, the rate had ascended to 81 percent, and by 1945 it towered at a confiscatory 94 percent level.

On rare occasions, the element of sanity does filter down into the halls of Congress. That is precisely what happened in 1952 when the maximum income tax was reduced to 92 percent. Again, the rate descended to 91 percent in 1963. It dropped to 77 percent in 1969. Today it stands at a still oppressive 70 percent.

While the rich have been getting soaked, the poor have not fared any better. The supporters of the income tax amendment could gloat in 1916 that the income tax only scissored away 27 percent as much money from the people as did the alcohol excise tax. They were gloating less, explaining more and committing the same basic errors in 1917 when the money dusted off the soon-to-be beleaguered taxpayers soared from 68 million dollars to 180 million.

The income tax scraped away 845 million dollars in 1925. The government pumped 982 million dollars out of the private economy in 1940. Ten years later, the IRS pillaged 17,000 *million* dollars from the sitting ducks who called America their home. In 1955, they peeled away 31,700 million dollars.

They seared us for 44,900 million dollars in 1960, and whittled away 53,700 million dollars in 1965. *The IRS gripped ahold of 103,600 million dollars in 1970.* They are now hooking us for 22 times as much money in income taxes as they are in alcohol excise taxes. The comparative tax burden has soared *eighty times* since 1916.

Well over a million times as much money is buccaneered away from the American taxpayer by government than was seized in the very first income tax.

Harpers magazine reports that Americans paid 16.7 billion dollars more in 1977 taxes than they did on the basic necessities of life -- food, clothing and shelter. The average American pays $79 more each year in per capita taxes than he does for the essentials he needs to stay alive.

Everyone knows that death and taxes are the only two sure things in life. Even the government knows it, so they devised a way to tax you when you die.

The first death tax was passed in 1797. The maximum tax was one half of one percent -- and it was completely abolished in 1802. Death duties re-appeared during the Spanish-American War. The most anyone had to pay was five percent, and the levy was phased out in a few years.

The death tax popped up for the last time in 1916 -- but **it** never died (there is always an exception to the rule). The maximum tax was ten percent. Just like the stories of social security and the income tax, the death tax rate floated higher and higher with each passing year.

Just a percentage point here and a percentage point there. Ever so slightly the maximum death tax grew. It has now broadened to the 77 percent level.

There is only one reason to have a death tax as sticking and precipitous as the one we have today -- and that is to give the social planners in Washington a tool with which to level wealth.

No where in the tax structure can there be found a more unfair, authoritarian or paternalistic attitude. Imagine the arrogance of a weasel - like bureaucrat -- a man whose life is spent swilling at the public trough -- prohibiting the productive citizen from giving way his property to the people he loves. The government wants **their** cut first -- and it can be as high as 77 percent.

The bureaucrats, politicians and tax collectors are to-day's sophisticated Luddites, destroying the wealth created by the productive through service to a market of free people. If all the loot marauded from the estates of peaceful citizens were used to run the federal government, the titanic monster would run out of fuel in less than four days. THEY DON'T EVEN NEED THE MONEY!

The story gets worse as the plot thickens.

Taxes assessed by state governments have risen even **faster** than federal taxes! State income taxes, for example, vaulted 400 percent **over the past decade alone!**

Reports from the Commerce Department show that state governments sunk a 101 billion dollar harpoon into the side of the American taxpayer in 1977. That was 13.2 percent more than the 89.3 billion dollars knifed away a year earlier. It was the first time in history they flaked us for more than 100 billion dollars.

Sales taxes brought in 51.8 percent of the heist. Personal state income taxes were responsible for 25.3 percent, corporate income taxes amounted to 9.1 percent, gasoline taxes made up 9 percent, and other miscellaneous sources took in 4.8 percent.

Minnesota and Wisconsin are head and shoulders at being the heaviest taxing states. They tax their citizens more than any other state does at every income bracket. Onerous thrashings are also doled out by Delaware, Oregon and Massachusetts. The four heaviest taxed cities are

New York, Boston, Buffalo and Chicago. Less crushing state tax burdens are imposed by Louisiana, Maine, Michigan, Nebraska, and Ohio. The four lightest taxed cities are Jacksonville, New Orleans, Houston and Atlanta.

While state income taxes blasted away 25.6 billion dollars, no income tax at all was levied in Connecticut, Florida, Nevada, South Dakota, Texas, Washington or Wyoming. New Hampshire and Tennessee only tax interest and dividends.

Less than six percent is badgered away from the residents of Arizona, Illinois, Indiana, Louisiana, Maryland, Michigan, Mississippi, Ohio, Pennsylvania, Rhode Island, Tennessee, Virginia and West Virginia.

The poorest Minnesota resident is burned out of 12.8 percent of his income, which is a higher rate than that confiscated from even the wealthiest citizen of any other state, save Delaware (in which case the single taxpayer earning more than $40,000 is 13.2 percent financially disrobed) and Vermont (where the couple earning more than $40,000 is flogged for 13.1 percent of their income, and a single is grated for 15 percent). The income from more prosperous Minnesotans is also mauled by 15 percent.

Every state in the Union has saddled its citizenry with a sales tax except Alaska, Delaware, Montana, New Hampshire and Oregon.

Without doubt, the biggest single act of piracy embarked upon by state and local governments has been the property tax. Local per capita property taxes averaged $88.39 in 1960. They were up 28 percent to $113.32 in 1965. They sprung another 43 percent in 1970 to $162.61. They bounced up 45 percent in 1978 to a whopping $235.77.

Property taxes increased an overall 167 percent during the post 1960 period. They now clear away almost one thousand dollars every year from the average family of four.

And there's more. Many cities have set up **municipal** income taxes. Included are Akron, Baltimore, Birmingham, Cincinnati, Cleveland, Columbus, Dayton, Detroit, Grand Rapids, Kansas City, Louisville, New York, Philadelphia, St. Louis, Washington, D.C. . .

So whether it's federal, state, county or municipal government, the message is abundantly clear: the taxpayer is being gouged, gored and gaffed at every turn.

"There was a time when a fool and his money were soon parted, but now it happens to everybody."
Adlai Stevenson

Chapter Three

THE MORALITY OF TAX AVOIDANCE

"Since man has to sustain his life by his own effort, the man who has no right to the product of his effort has no means to sustain his life. The man who produces while others dispose of his product is a slave."

Ayn Rand

Two hundred years ago, the King of England imposed the Sugar Act of 1964 on the American colonies. It had the effect of placing an excise tax on foodstuffs, lumber, molasses and rum. The taxes were used to quarter the King's army inside American homes, a use the colonists strongly objected to.

In reaction, British goods were boycotted across America. The Sons of Liberty organization was born, and numerous chapters were chartered. Nine colonies formed the Stamp Act Congress, which drew up a declaration of rights and urged repeal of the Stamp Act.

Patrick Henry warned the King of the brewing tax revolt when he exclaimed, "If this be treason, let us make the most of it". In 1766, the tax was rescinded.

The next year brought the Townshend Act and its taxes on printers lead, paper, glass and tea. All tax duties, except the tax on tea, were repealed in 1770. And it was that one tax which spawned the American Revolution. Imagine, a revolution erupting over one tax. The tax was assessed on a luxury good and, by today's standards, the burden was certainly within tolerable limits. Why raise such a fuss? Today's tax-encumbered American would gladly trade places with even the most angry of the colonists.

The reason a fuss was raised was because the American Revolution was driven by a principle. The patriots fueled their zeal to fight with the **idea** that there are certain inalienable rights (rights which cannot be taken away) possessed by every living and breathing human being. They knew man possessed these rights by virtue of being an individual. A man's rights were his when he was born and his when he died. Rights, the colonists knew, are innate. Rights are not granted by government. Anything that was granted, reasoned the patriots, can also be taken away. Anything approved can be revoked. Man's rights resided within the individual.

It was this zeal for individual rights that fired Patrick Henry into proclaiming, "Give me liberty or give me death". Patrick Henry knew that a man had rights that could not be taken away from him by government. Government had no moral authority to intrude, meddle or coerce. It had no moral authority to tax a free people. Patrick Henry didn't risk his life because he was annoyed at the increased price of tea. He knew that when government had the authority to tax, the only question that remained was how high that tax might be. It was the principle of taxation that worried Patrick Henry and his retinue of friends. If empowered with the ability to seize private holdings by force of law, government might one day be able to tax a man out of his home.

Notions such as these seeped and percolated inside the minds of those men who drafted the Declaration of Independence. About government, the document stated, "When a long train of abuses and usurpations evinces a design to reduce them under absolute despotism, it is their right, it is their duty, to throw off such a government and to provide new guards for their future security". Dissatisfaction with the King's government was expressed as the patriots wrote, "for imposing taxes on us without our consent". In disapproval of the teams of government bureaucrats sent over from England to regulate the colonists, they wrote of the King, "He has erected a multitude of new offices and sent hither swarms of officers to harass our people and eat out their substance".

The Declaration of Independence was a document opposed to the force and coercion of government against peaceful individuals. The Declaration was addressed to a monarchy, but it was just as applicable to a dictatorship, aristocracy, oligarchy, democracy or even a republic without a constitution. What the patriots wanted was a small, limited government that would leave them alone in peace and secure the protection of life, liberty and property.

Man's individual integrity was discovered in 1776, and the principle that he is endowed with individual rights that cannot be taken away from him by government is as valid today as it was 200 years ago. Every human being has the absolute right to his life. His life is his own to do with as he pleases. It wasn't given to him by government and no one except himself has the right to take it away. Rights entail the duty of forbearance. You have a right to your life; likewise, your neighbor has a right to **his** life. You have no right to take his life away. If you have the right to your own life, you have a duty to refrain from violating the equal rights others have to their lives.

If an individual has a right to his life, he has an equal right to sustain that life. He may act upon the alternatives presented to him in the world, but he may not use force to achieve his objectives. To do so would abridge the equal rights of others.

The individual may only choose the alternatives that **don't** interfere with the rights of others. This is accomplished in human society when human interaction is voluntary. The voluntary society only produces associations when both people want to associate. Each individual is free to do as he pleases. If one person does not wish to associate, the association does not take place. The meaning of liberty is this ability of individuals in society to exercise free choice in determining what they will do and with whom they will do it.

Rights are abridged whenever someone is required to do something against his will -- whenever an association ceases to be voluntary. "Force" is the name given to the unwilling involvement thrust upon another person. Where there is force, there is no voluntary association, and where there is an involuntary association, there is a case of "unequal" rights. Wherever there is force or coercion, individual rights are being violated.

Free trade is merely an extension of the voluntary society characterized by liberty. Two items are exchanged under free trade because each trader would rather have what the other one has. A voluntary exchange takes place because each trader values the object held by the other trader more highly than he does the object he holds. Each trader can benefit by trading. The exchange takes place because both parties benefit. If only **one** of the traders didn't feel that he would benefit by trading, he wouldn't trade.

Free trade is mutually beneficial to the trading partners. As such, it is additively beneficial to society as a whole. No force is involved with free trade -- just choice. Free trade is a voluntary association of free people with equal rights. If man has the right to liberty (equal rights, free choice and voluntary association), the authority to make decisions resides in the individual. He has control over the choices he is faced with. If the things an individual controls may be thought of as the things he owns, and if the things a person owns may be defined as his property, he has the right to control the things he owns. He has an absolute right to his property.

Economic freedom is based on the right to own and exchange property. It is a combination of property rights and free trade. Economic freedom implies that if any profit is made in a voluntary economic association, the profit becomes the property of the individual who earns it. Every man's body is his own property -- because he owns and controls his own life. Every man has a right to the income he earns from his property. Whether that income is classified as wages, salaries, commissions, interest, royalties, rents, dividends or profits, the income rightfully belongs to the individual as owner of the income-generating property.

The thinkers behind the Revolution knew what they were saying when declaring man has a right to life, liberty and property.

Theft is the involuntary appropriation of someone else's property. It is a clear violation of property rights. It is not hard to see that the man on the street who asks people for money and accosts them when they don't hand it over is a thief. He is no less a thief if he joins a gang who extorts money from small businessmen unless they hand over "protection money". Theft is theft is theft, whether there are one, two or three dozen thieves.

What if there are 80,000 thieves working together in the same gang? Of course, the money this gang takes is also theft. What if this gang somehow infiltrates into the government and is granted legal immunity from plundering the property of innocent victims? Don't become alarmed, but it has already happened. The large gang is known as the Internal Revenue Service. It has a bevy of 80,000 thugs who are euphemistically called agents, auditors or bureaucrats. The gang seizes money to satisfy the alleged debts it says we, the unfortunate victims, owe. The pilferage should be called larceny, theft, robbery, booty or loot. But it goes under the alternate headings of tax, duty, levy or assessment.

Be sure of one thing -- taxation is legally sanctioned theft. It is a frightening proposition because taxation presumes the legal authority of government to take away a large part of the money that is rightfully yours. Once granted the power to tax, government is authorized to tax away as much as it wants. All it has to do is pass a law.

A prisoner was pictured in a recent cartoon asking his cellmate why he was incarcerated. The cellmate answered, "For riding with a gang of robbers who terrorized the countryside. How about you?" "I was a Congressman," the prisoner replied. "Can I ride with **you** next time?" queried the cellmate.

Government determines the "tax rate". Under taxation, the government has first claim on the individual citizen's earnings. If government determines how much money the individual may keep, government controls his material sustenance. The individual exists under permission of the government and must submit to their edicts. Government has violated the right to life and makes every taxpayer a government slave.

The most obvious transgression of taxation is the violation of the right to property. The money you earn and the assets you own are rightfully yours, but the government "passes a law" and claims part of your property as its own; and if you don't pony up, they indict **you** as the criminal. The tax laws have totally inverted the meaning of justice, which brings us to the morality of tax avoidance.

As we have already seen, taxation is grostesquely immoral. Not only is it the biggest scam known to hit civilization, but it is used for highly destructive purposes. Taxation is what's used to finance political wars and the countless other vehicles used by prevaricating politicians to rub their egos, achieve fame and glory, steal money and grab power. Taxation has made possible devastating social programs, ridiculous research grants, boondoggles, welfare and waste. Fast buck bureaucrats, politicians and tax collectors have shoved a fiscal siphon into the veins of the private economy and opened wide the spigot to drain the productive sector of its output. The economic vampires in Washington have then poured the sluice into a non-productive, all-consuming bureaucracy that not only feeds like a leech on productive citizens but devotes every waking hour thinking of new ways to intrude, meddle and regulate the activities of private citizens.

The political tax bureaucracy has grown into a bloated bloodsucker. It continues to grow, becomes more expensive, more demanding and less intelligible. Government is destroying the prosperity and freedom enjoyed by our society.

The governmental gargantua can be stopped if the flood of dollars gushing into our nation's capitol were slowed to a trickle. Without the inebriating over-abundance of money, the fuddlers, lushes and sots in charge of public policy would be forced to trim expenditures. In doing so, they might even take a couple of weights off the neck of productive society. It took a revolution in 1978 -- California's Proposition 13 (an unlucky number for the politicians) taxpayer's revolt, just to get the attention of the politicians and bureaucrats.

Estimates show the average American taxpayer could reduce his taxes by as much as 25 percent with a well-planned, comprehensive tax strategy. That's because the average American **overpays** his taxes by as much as 25 percent. If everyone were to pay the least possible taxes he had to, the dollar flow to Washington could be choked off by as much as 25 percent.

You have a responsibility to yourself to lessen the crushing burden of oppressive taxation. Taxation is theft, which means you have a moral obligation to do whatever you can to mitigate the volume of taxes scraped away from you by the government. You must safeguard the money that is rightfully yours.

What follows is a guide to help you forge your own personal tax strategy. How much you can avoid paying depends on how well you understand your tax options.

Will you keep your money or will you entrust it to the government? The bureaucrats, politicians and tax collectors have done absolutely nothing in the past to merit your trust, and they promise to use whatever you give them in the way you disapprove of most.

Small limited government, a free market economy and a society protective of individual rights can be achieved if the size and scope of government is reduced. We can make them stop prying into our personal lives if we just cut off their supply of food. The only solution is to cut taxes, and it can be done without even passing a single law. So get out your scratch pad and sharpen your pencil. Take careful notes. Here is a way you can save yourself some money, pinch the tax suction tube and advance the cause of liberty in one fell swoop!

"Money is power. Money in your hands is power in you. In the hands of the government, it gives the government power over you. Governments never use unlimited money for good. They quickly convert it to unlimited power. And unlimited power in any government is oppression for all."

T. Coleman Andrews
Former Commissioner of
Internal Revenue

PART II

STOPPING THE TAX MILL

"Tax evasion is illegal; tax avoidance is not. Every tax-payer has a right to adjust his affairs so that he minimizes his tax liability. He can avoid the payment of higher taxes by so adjusting his affairs as to make his transactions subject to some lesser tax bracket. We recognize such steps as perfectly legitimate business undertakings."

Russell C. Harrington
Commissioner of Internal Revenue

Chapter Four

KNOW THE IRS

"There is nothing sinister in so arranging one's affairs to keep taxes as low as possible. Everyone does so, rich or poor, and all do right, for nobody owes any public duty to pay more tax than the law demands; taxes are enforced exactions, not voluntary contributions. To demand more in the name of morals is mere cant."

Judge Learned Hand

(Any relation, do you suppose, to Adam Smith's INVISIBLE hand?)

Proceed with caution. The government is armed and dangerous. Before you start exploring the different possibilities of ways to ease your tax bite, you should examine some of the statistics and descriptive information concerning the spongers inside the IRS.

While the leviathan tax agency has 80,000 agents in its employ and towers above the pygmy-sized taxpayer in financial resources, information retrieval abilities, legal expertise and experience, you shouldn't lose sight of the fact that the IRS is dwarfed by the 1,000 taxpayers that exist for every IRS employee.

Only one out of every five IRS employees is an outside agent, and only a very small fraction are auditors. While it is true that the IRS could gun down any one of us if it took the notion to marshall all of its vast resources in our direction, it should be of some solace to you that the IRS is even more badly outnumbered than is the starcrossed tax payer.

In pursuit of IRS policy, which seems to say "pluck as many feathers from the public goose with the least possible amount of hissing", much of the contentious attitude displayed by the IRS is grounded on bluff and intimidation. While present law allows the IRS to confiscate every thing a delinquent taxpayer owns except $500 in private property and $250 in business property, IRS managers place heavy pressure on their employees to process as many audits as they can. The whole purpose of auditing you is to sink their teeth deeper into your pocket book. Their job performance is monitored on the basis of how much additional money they can shuck out of the weary taxpayer.

As a result, you should keep in mind the fact that the auditor is prodded with incentives to finish each individual case as quickly as possible. The taxpayer will pose more trouble to the auditor's quota and be more likely to emerge unscathed the longer he can delay the auditor, the more he can bog the auditor down, the more adamant and valid the taxpayer is in his choice of a tax strategy, the more obstinate the taxpayer is to agreeing with any "compromise" settlement, and the more persistant he is with every claim.

This is not to suggest the taxpayer should be obnoxious. Belligerance against the IRS would be more effectively vented at another, more opportune, time. Be firm and businesslike. Refrain from being overly courteous. Don't give the tax agent any more records than he asks for. Avoid idle conversation like you would avoid leprosy, and don't take the agent to lunch. If you have employees, bar them from addressing the IRS agent any more than is absolutely necessary. Isolate the agent such that he is left alone and exposed. Maintain a cold and sterile environment. Keep written track of the records the agent looks at. Record the kinds of questions he asks. By all means, don't enlighten the agent with your opinions about the government or the IRS. There will be plenty of time for that after the audit.

Studies have shown that low income taxpayers make fertile targets for the IRS. Low income taxpayers can't afford expensive lawyers and their returns are comparatively simple. The outcome of the audit often hinges on a couple all-or-nothing disputes.

The IRS wins 62 percent of the contested claims against those who earn less than $10,000. But they only win 51 percent of the claims contested by people earning between $10,000 and $50,000. Guess who they go after. Like a hunter in search of prey, the quota-studded auditing managers turn their agents loose on the returns filed by people in the lower income brackets, which require less manpower due to their non-complex nature. While 3.6 percent of the lower income taxpayers were audited in 1974, only 2.4 percent of the people in the more affluent category were scrutinized. This means your chances of being investigated by an audit are 50 percent greater if you are less well off.

The intimidating choice of psychologically terrorizing words inside the instruction manuals to IRS forms is another example of the bluff behind the Internal Revenue Service. No word is peppered throughout the manuals with greater frequency than is "must". Following close behind for a photofinish second is "required". Then come phrases like "does not", "shall not", "may not", and "never".

While the instructions talk about the financial drubbing you can see starting to take firm, the tone is magisterial and authoritative. When reflecting on what the pallid taxpayer can do to minimize the rip tide of taxes, the language takes a sudden turn and becomes ambiguous, loose and tenuous. One way to circumnavigate the biases riddled throughout IRS propaganda is to read their information with the prior understanding that the pamphlets are deliberately designed to evoke anxiety and instill fear of the IRS.

Whenever you see the word "never", substitute in your mind the word "rarely". The word "must" is translated to mean "according to the IRS". And "may" is interpreted to mean "this is what to do to save taxes".

The belief the IRS is omniscient in the sphere of tax knowledge is one of the most widespread fallacies. Several years ago the IRS conducted an experiment. It sent some of its agents into IRS offices to pose as taxpayers in search of answers to some fairly basic questions. Seven out of ten times the answers they got back from the IRS were wrong. Most of the errors were in the government's favor, and for every two dollar mistake in favor of the tax-payer, there was a three dollar mistake in favor of the IRS. There is a sea of Bimbos floating in the IRS soup. They can't give you any straight answer you can rely on. The odds of getting favorable treatment are better in Las Vegas.

Less complex returns are generally assigned to inexperienced tax auditors. Then is when you can hear the air filled with the highest density of bull, buncombe and bureaucrateze. The green horn auditor will flex his intimidating legal muscles with much more enthusiasm than does a seasoned agent. He will make absurd statements you should be prepared to trump. Call every bluff. The IRS relies heavily on fear. They can jail you or hook you for nearly everything you own. They are the judge, jury, prosecutor and warden. The cloak of law they don instills the same fear we experience in the near vicinity of a wild animal that has the capacity to lacerate us to death.

You will be in no position to effectively save on taxes if you succomb to the terrorist tactics of the IRS. The whole purpose behind the wide and varied assortment of intimidation practices is to make you docile, passive and manageable.

The IRS has rightfully earned a predatory reputation for its dogged persistance in clinging to highly dubious practices and interpretations of the tax law. They have dragged taxpayers into court across different parts of the country for the sole purpose of getting different decisions from which to appeal and re-appeal a case all the way to the

Supreme Court (by which time the combative taxpayer is worn out). Sometimes, the delirious taxpayer even loses when he wins.

Industrialist Vivian Kellems is a prime example. She valiantly refused to deduct withholding taxes from her workers in 1948 and challenged the government to indict her in their own courts, fair and square. Her purpose was to test the constitutionality of the withholding system. Instead, the government snatched the money from her private bank account. She sued and got her money back three years later — less than a constitutional test. When Mrs. Kellems passed away in 1978, a pack of IRS cutthroats foraged through her defenseless estate.

The taxpayer should be aware of some of the alternatives available to him. If the dispute with the IRS is for an amount smaller than $1,500, the case may be taken to the small claims tax court, where the atmosphere is informal and the decisions don't set precedents. The decisions in small claims court are final. The only catch is that the IRS must ok the transferral of the case's settlement.

Two basic options face cases where the contested amount exceeds $1,500. If you reluctantly pay the tax and sue for a refund, your case will first be heard in the U.S. Court of Claims or one of the federal district courts. Either of these trials tend to be less harsh than the second option, which is to forgo paying the tax until after the final declaration of judgment but have the case argued before the Tax Court. The taxpayer who knows he has a weak case may intentionally gum up the settlement for several years at modest cost. If he has the intestonal fortitude to weather the IRS into a Mexican standoff for a sufficient length of time, the taxpayer might even bargain himself into getting some major concessions out of the IRS. The worst that could happen is that he could use his money longer and draw interest. That's better than a poke in the eye.

Much of the omnipotent presence the IRS throws around is illusive balderdash. They cannot possibly see, know and hear everything. The 1099 form, for example, serves the purpose of fostering an impression that the IRS keeps track of every nickel, dime and quarter of what they disparagingly refer to as "unearned" income (dividends and interest). IRS officials send out press releases describing the elaborate computer systems that supposedly catch tax evaders with uncanny infallibility. The actual truth of the matter is that only one out of every 40 returns is audited, and only a few ever amount to anything. The fear propaganda issued with calculated timing by the IRS is not much more than near-empty chatter. The sooner the taxpayer can peek around the magnifying glass and realize the projected image of the IRS as formidable beast is nothing but a hype-produced illusion, the sooner he can convert his docility into confident self-willed defiance. Once you have the courage, you can prick the inflated balloon of IRS exaggerations, release the hot air, see beneath the tax idiom and use a strategy to minimize the erosion of your property by the covey of flimflam men running the IRS shell game.

"In a recent conversation with an official of the Internal Revenue Service, I was amazed when he told me that if the

taxpayers of this country ever discovered that the Internal Revenue Service operates on 90 percent bluff, the entire system would collapse."

Senator Henry Bellmon

CHAPTER FIVE

THE PRELIMINARIES

"The legal right of a taxpayer to decrease the amount of what otherwise would be his taxes, or to altogether avoid them by means which the law permits cannot be doubted."
                                                    U. S. Courts

The first determination a taxpayer must make when filing his income tax return is his filing status. It is not always cheaper for married couples to file joint returns. If both husband and wife earn comparable incomes, they save little in filing jointing and could end up on the short end of the stick in lost deductions. It is hard to know whether or not a married couple should file a joint return or two single returns. The only sure way to find out is by figuring out both tax totals and filing with the status yielding the lower tax.

The head of the household does not have to be the same person every year, so if the wife earns more than the husband, it may lessen the tax burden by listing her as head of the household.

An individual may file as an unmarried head of a household rather than as a single if he pays more than half the amount of maintaining a household, the household is the principal residence of a dependent relative and the taxpayer was unmarried on December 31 of the tax year.

A $750 exemption may be claimed for each dependent. You may only count dependents who earn less than $750 in taxable income and who receive more than half their support from you. The dependent must be a U. S. Citizen and must not have filed a joint return. Any close relatives may qualify as a dependent. So may any unrelated person, if he has lived with you for a year.

The Presidential election Campaign Fund will not affect your taxes. By approving the designation of a dollar from general tax revenues to help finance the election, you will contribute toward the public financing of presidential campaigns.

Will Rogers once said, "This country has gotten where it is in spite of politics, not by the aid of it". Public financing removes the influence of those segments of the population who are few in number yet strong in their beliefs. It circumvents the cornerstone of the principles behind a free and open democracy — namely, the free marketplace of ideas. It gives free reign to the populist demogogues who are in search of fortunes to pilfer, ravish and plunder. If for no other reason than this, it is highly recommended that you *don't* contribute to their little lottery. Don't donate — it only encourages them. It may only be a dollar, but it is a dollar that will help the politicians convert the promises of today into the taxes of tomorrow. Don't help them do it.

An important question always pondered by the taxpayer is the issue of deductions. Should you itemize or should you use the standard deduction? The answer, of course, is to do whatever minimizes the devastation of your income by the Internal Revenue Service.

If you are filing jointly, you will save money by itemizing if your adjusted gross income is less than $11,875 and you have more than $1,900 in itemized deductions. You will save by itemizing if you earn between $11,875 and $16,250 and if your deductions come to more than 16 percent of your income. If you earn more than $16,250, you will save money by itemizing if you have more than $2,600 in deductions.

If you are single, or if you are unmarried head of a household, you will benefit by itemizing if your adjusted gross income is less than $10,000 and if your itemized deductions are more than $1,600. You will come out ahead by itemizing if you earn between $10,000 and $14,375 and your itemized deductions are more than 16 percent of your income. If you earn more than $14,375 and you have more than $2,300 in itemized deductions, you will be doing yourself a favor by itemizing.

No legitimate expense may be deducted unless it is backed up with iron-plated proof. If you don't adequately protect yourself, you are being exposed to an IRS broadside.

One simple way to get into the record-keeping habit is to use the fish bowl accounting method. It's simple. All you have to do is write down the date, amount and purpose on the back of every receipt you get. Tuck the receipt into a convenient carrying spot and throw it into an empty fish bowl when you get home. Make sure to circle the taxes you pay at the grocers and toss those receipts in, too. It is amazing how quickly the receipts will accumulate and how apparently "insignificant" expenses will get you a couple extra hundred dollars in deductions.

You can simplify the documentation process and categorize your expenses by using credit cards. Save the monthly statements and receipts. Credit cards are excellent vehicles to use in segregating expenses. Master Charge can be used for household costs; Visa for business expenses; American Express for travel; Diners Club for entertainment; and oil company cards for gas. The list is endless. Checking accounts at separate banks provide the same documentation vehicles.

Some people carry scratch pads with them, like they carry a watch or wallet. They carefully scribble down every expense, assiduously noting taxes. Not only does it develop thrifty habits, but it produces a punctilious record upon which you can base future deductions.

Keep all records a *minimum* of three years. That's when the statute of limitations runs out. All capital records should be permanent and indelible, whether they are investments in stocks, bonds, limited partnership or real estate. Keep a photocopy of every tax return in a permanent file just in case you ever have to income average or if the IRS loses your return. The IRS, while scrupulously diligent in lassoing, tying up and roping off our hard-earned money, is quite careless with the confidential records we are forced to turn over to them. In fact, the Internal Revenue Service loses more pages than many bureaucracies churn out! The IRS mandates that every record be permanent, accurate and complete. They have been known to disallow deductions that later proved to be allowed solely on the basis of what they termed "inadequate substantiating records".

The bunco artist at Internal Revenue will only accept cancelled checks and bills stamped "paid" as expense records. It is highly recommended that you write any information on the check entry that proves the expense is deductible.

Keep separate accounts and files for personal and business expenses. Take special care to substantiate any travel entertainment or gift expenditures serving a business purpose. Make sure to write down the amount, the purpose, the business relationship of the person entertained or the individual presented the gift, the time date and place of the entertainment, travel or gift. What's required by the IRS is documentary evidence proving the amount, date, time, place, purpose and essential character of the business expense. If you keep proper records and use a valid tax-cutting strategy, you should be able to safely minimize your taxes to the lowest possible extent. If audited, you should have nothing to fear.

The desperados in the IRS are constantly examining the skeletal remains of the wasted American taxpayer. Like bugs at the end of a pin, they process, computerize and gobble at endless lengths, lying awake nights thinking of ways to milk us even more dry than they already have. What they have come up with after intruding into our privacy with ruminating persistence is a set of "averages". If your deductions deviate away from the averages to any appreciable extent, you become an instant candidate for a tax audit. So examine the data the IRS has gathered on us. The unblinking eyes of their computers are set to spot variations and identify the "abnormal" returns.

Low income taxpayers (those whose adjusted gross income lies between $5,000 and $10,000) are expected to claim deductions amounting to 41.2 percent of their income. The IRS predicts medical expenses will consume an average 11.5 percent of income. Taxes are expected to swipe 10.6 percent. Interest payments, says the IRS, should take away 14.1 percent. Contributions usually account for 5 percent.

The middle income taxpayer earning between $10,000 and $25,000 spends an average 3.2 percent of his income on medical expense. He is mulcted out of 8.3 percent of his income, thanks to other taxes. Interest removes 8.8 percent out of his pocket, and he contributes 2.7 percent to charity. Another 2 percent goes toward miscellaneous deductions. As a result, the IRS expects 25 percent of the middle income taxpayer to be consumed by allowable deductions.

The ill-fated upper income taxpayer (earning between $25,000 and $100,000) is only expected to deduct 19 percent out of his adjusted gross income. As might be expected 7.5 percent — the largest figure — is due to the fusillades leveled at him by the other levels of government. An expected 1.2 percent is tagged for medical expenses and 5.9 percent for interest payments. The more prosperous citizen contributes 2.5 percent of his money to deductible charities, with 1.9 percent expected for miscellaneous deductions.

"To be governed is to be watched, inspected, spied upon, directed, preached at, checked, appraised, seized, censured, commanded by beings who have neither title nor knowledge nor virtues. To be governed is to have every movement noted, registered, counted, rated, stamped, measured, numbered, assessed, licensed, refused, authorized, endorsed, admonished, prevented, reformed, redressed, corrected."

Proudhon

CHAPTER SIX

THE BASIC DEDUCTIONS

"Bribes and kickbacks to non-governmental officials are deductible unless the individual has been convicted of making the bribe or has entered a plea of nolo contendere."
1971 Federal Income Tax Form

Every year, the Treasury Department submits a report to Congress called "Tax Expenditures". These are the taxes which were not scoured from taxpayers because of legal deductions written into the IRS code. The government sees everything they let us deduct as an "expenditure". As the covetous IRS sees it, we are working for them and they are throwing us an occasional bone to keep us working. They see the remainder of our income as government property. Your purpose is to use the tax systems' framework to make sure that bone is as large as possible.

The slavemasters at the IRS won't let you deduct any medical or dental expense unless they amount to 3 percent or more of your adjusted gross income. It should be noted that most people earning more than $25,000 can't qualify; and the same goes for almost half the people earning a middle income of between $10,000 and $25,000 a year. They will, however, let you deduct half the premium for your hospitalization insurance, up to $150, irrespective of the 3 percent rule.

Income taxes, sales taxes, property taxes, gas taxes and

taxes on personal property slapped on the dupes who go under the heading of "taxpayer" by local or state governments are deductible. The taxes must have been imposed on you, and you must have paid them during the last tax year.

General sales tax tables for every state can be found inside the 1040 instructions. The amount they allow you to deduct without substantiating your receipts is based on both your adjusted gross income and on the number of dependents you have. If you use the simple fish bowl accounting method, you should add up the taxes you paid and compare them against the actuarial figures given to you by the IRS. Deduct whichever one is largest. Keep in mind, however, that the general sales tax allowance listed in the IRS general tables does not include five additional sales taxes that may be deducted even if you use the general tables. You may deduct the sales tax you pay when buying a boat, car, airplane, mobile home or the construction materials you use in building your own house.

The government pillagers will let you deduct just about any tax except FEDERAL TAXES. These include withholding taxes, social security taxes, custom duties, estate taxes, gift taxes or federal excise taxes on motor vehicles, air transportation, telephone service or tires. Nor will the swindlers let you deduct state or local taxes on inheritance or gift taxes, cigarette taxes, tobacco taxes or taxes on alcoholic drinks. They won't let you deduct fees for automobile inspections, tolls, dog tags, marriage licenses, car licenses, hunting license or parking meters. The rogues will not let you deduct the interest you pay when borrowing money to buy tax-free bonds or single-premium life insurance policies.

But you *can* deduct the interest you pay on charge accounts. Make sure you keep the monthly statements as proof. Most other interest payments are deductible, including that which accrues on unpaid taxes.

Casualty and theft losses are deductible in full if they are incurred by a business. Losses over $100 may be deducted by individuals.

Child care and dependent care services are deductible up to $400 a month. Expenses are limited to $200 per month for one child, $300 for two children and $400 for three or more children. The costs for nursery school or day care qualify as child care expenses. Related household costs like wages paid to maid, housekeeper, nurse or cook are also deductible.

The rancorous IRS requires that the taxpayer file form 2441 if he has expenses for household and dependent care services. He must also list the total on schedule A, which is normally attached to the 1040 form. Expenses must be employment-related to qualify, which means they are expenses you have to pay in order to stay employed.

Employee business expenses are yet another fertile source of deductions. All of an employee's work-related travel and transportation expenses are deductible — except the costs of commuting between home and place of business. You can deduct gasoline, road tolls, a car mileage allowance, valet expenses, subway fares, telephone and telegraph charges, food and lodging, laundry, tips and many other items. The list goes on into outer space.

Car expenses are perhaps the largest employee business expense. You can either use the 15¢ per mile allowance for the first 15,000 miles and 10¢ per mile afterwards, or you can actually figure out the costs. It takes more time, but you will probably come out ahead. Remember that car expenses include depreciation (which can be substantial for a new car), gas, oil, insurance, state and local taxes, license and registration fees and maintenance costs like tires, repairs, tune-ups, fan belts, batteries, car washes, lights anti-freeze, brakes and windshield wipers . . . .

You may deduct entertainment expenses and an employee business expense, if you can document that you are required by your employer to entertain as a part of your job. A letter from your boss substantiating your employment obligation lends enormous credibility to any claim you make for an entertainment expense. The importance of substantiating your entertainment deductions with proper records should be emphasized once again. The business purpose of the expense should be recorded. It should cultivate goodwill, produce new business, maintain old business, make a sale, etc.

Gifts may be deducted if they are business-related and cost less than $25.

When entertaining business associates, you can write off the cost of your wife's meal. When you take your wife along on business, however, the IRS snoops prohibit you from deducting the full cost of your motel room. You can write-off half the motel bill, if you wish, but there is yet a better option available to you, if you want to save a few extra dollars. Find out and document the single occupancy rate and deduct the amount you would have spent had you slept alone.

Record the actual business purpose served of every business-related dinner, convention or party. If you can demonstrate a purpose, you can rest easy in the event you are actually audited.

Some acceptable employee expenses are employment agency fees, magazine and newspaper subscriptions, professional club dues and initiation fees, employer-required physical examination, malpractice premiums and educational expenses needed to maintain your job.

The Internal Revenue Service will also let you write off all income-producing expenses such as the expenses of an income-producing hobby. They'll let you write off appraisal fees, tax assistance (like the cost of this book) alimony and up to $100 in political contributions (with a joint return.)

They have not permitted us to deduct burial expenses, lost money, tax fines, non-medical insurance, personal legal expenses, home repairs or rent.

Moving expenses are another item that may be used to reduce your reportable, taxable income. To qualify, your new work location must be at least fifty miles farther from your old house than from your old work location. If you had to travel ten miles from your old house to your old place of work, it must be sixty or more miles from your old house to your new place of work to qualify your moving expenses as deductible costs. You also must be employed for 39 weeks or more out of the 12 month period following your move. If you work for yourself, the IRS devised an even harsher set of rules you should know about. Not only does the God-forsaken entrepreneur have to work 39 out of the first 52 weeks, but he has to put in 78 weeks of work time over a two year period as well.

Include every item that is permitted as a moving expense. Don't forget travel expenses, such as meals and lodging for your family in transit between homes. You can either write off the actual driving costs or you can deduct the monstrous sum of six cents per mile.

Don't forget the costs for transportation, packing, crating, in-transit storage and insurance. You can write off the cost for meals and lodging at temporary facilities for thirty days. The Picaroons at Internal Revenue will only let you deduct one-way travel, meals and lodging expenses for pre-move househunting trips. They'll let you write-off the cost of the return trip after you start working at the new location. You can deduct the lawyer and appraisal fees as well as escrow and title costs on the new home you buy. You can write off real estate commissions, state transfer taxes, points and lawyer, title and escrow fees on the old home you sell.

All costs borne to settle a lease may be deducted, whether you are closing out an old lease or opening up a new one.

And finally, you can deduct a part of the sick pay you receive. The rules regarding sick pay exclusion are changing all the time, and the taxpayer who wants to see less of his property maimed by a rabid tax system should file Sick Pay Exclusion Form 2440.

The tricksters at the IRS have only one objective in life — to separate you from your rightful property. The vicious game they play is for keeps. Your financial well-being in the jungle of complex tax laws boils down to a matter of survival. Keep careful records. Maximize your deductions. Start formulating a tax minimization strategy.

"Anyone may so arrange his affairs that his taxes shall be as low as possible. He is not bound to choose that pattern which will best pay the Treasury; there is not even a patriotic duty to increase one's taxes."

Judge Learned Hand

CHAPTER SEVEN

SWEET CHARITY

"Behold, a glutton and a drunkard, a friend of tax collectors and sinners!"

Matthew 11:19

It only costs the churches eight cents to distribute a dollar of charity to the needy. Private charities average 28 cents in distribution costs for every dollar that is given away. The federal government spends three dollars in distribution costs for every initial dollar it spends.

When it comes time to contribute money to charity, you should pursue the approach that maximizes your freedom to give away as much as you want, to whomever you choose. Taxes stand in the way of this freedom. You are forced to use the tax structure to further your interests as best as you can. How well you can manipulate the regulations will determine how much of your money can be given away to those you want to have it, without the mischievous IRS busybodies nabbing a portion for themselves.

It is amazing how the IRS has been able to so successfully byzantify the simple act of charity into a baffling, perplexing and involuted knot of bibble-babble. Take, as one example, the car expenses you incur when you donate your time to charity. Of course, they'll let you deduct your car expenses, but what mileage rate do you suppose they will let you use? Is it the 15 cents per mile rate they apply to business car expenses or the 10 cents per mile rate they apply after a business car has travelled more than 15,000 miles in a single year? Or do they apply the same 6 cents per mile charge that applies when you are moving? The answer, as you might expect, is none of the above. For the sake of added complexity, the muttonheads have decreed that a special 7 cents per mile rate be used for charity purposes.

We are no longer taught the three R's in school. What we learn are the three C's taught us by the IRS once we get out — confusion, complexity and confabulation. While "Ten Four" is universally known by everyone as CB lingo for "message received and understood — over and out", "Ten Forty" is IRS lingo for "message received but too complex and incomprehensible. Instructions unclear, muddled and impenetrable. *Over and out*".

There are three charitable deduction rules: the 50 percent rule, the 30 percent rule and the 20 percent rule. You can give up to 50 percent of your adjusted gross income to charities if contributions are in the form of cash (hence the 50 percent rule). But if property which has appreciated in value is donated, the limit drops to 30 percent. If the cash or property gift is given to a private foundation, the limit drops to 20 percent.

The deductions that qualify under the 50 percent rule must be used first. Only then can you deduct those under the 20 percent rule. Last comes deductions under the 30 percent rule. You can carry forward contributions falling under the 50 and 30 percent rules for five years. The IRS flimflam men prohibit any carryovers at all for the 20 percent rule.

When the donor gives away tangible real property that, if sold, would have produced a long term capital gain, half the capital appreciation will be "disallowed" by the IRS unless the property will directly further the tax exempt purposes of the charity.

The recognized amount of a property gift is its fair market value. You can many times maximize your donation by giving property instead of cash. If you bought a piece of land ten years ago for $10,000 and it is now worth $25,000, and if you are in the 30 percent tax bracket, you could give that land to your favorite foundation and they could sell it for $25,000. If you sold it instead and gave them the cash, you would have to pay taxes on your $15,000 long term capital gains. Since only half of long term capital gains are taxed, you would owe taxes on $7,500; and since you would be in the 30 percent tax bracket, that means $2,250 would be diced away by the IRS strong man, which means you could only give away $22,750.

While charity may take the form of outright gifts, there are yet other methods of using a charitable vehicle for more effective tax savings. Many of these methods fall under the general category of gifts in trust.

A trust is used whenever an individual wishes to bestow a gift upon someone else but doesn't want to immediately dispose title of the assets. While a will directly and immediately transfers ownership, a trust does it after a period of time. Actual title to the property placed in a trust is vested in a trustee, who administers it for someone else's benefit. Care should be taken to select a responsible trustee who will perform his task with impartiality and integrity. A good choice often lies within the trust department of a bank.

Trusts may be used to reduce both income taxes and estate taxes. This chapter focuses on the use of charitable trusts to generate tax deductions, which reduce taxable income and deflate the fiscal injury of taxation. The next chapter pursues the use of trusts in softening the tax chops delivered by the estate managers of the IRS slaughterhouse.

The tax benefits are the primary reasons you have to give away your property to charity through a trust. Don't even consider setting up a charitable trust unless you actually intend to give away your property to charity. You should skip the rest of this chapter if your intentions lie elsewhere. Charitable trusts enable you to come out ahead because they use charity as a vehicle to reduce your income taxes.

There are two kinds of charitable trusts: annuity trusts and unitrusts. Both must make payments to a beneficiary at least once a year. Neither can last more than twenty years. Both trusts are indelibly irrevocable, and the government requires that the trust's assets ultimately be given away to charity.

Annuity trusts pay a fixed dollar amount to the beneficiary. The trust's assets are given to a charity when the trust expires. A unitrust pays to the beneficiary a fixed percentage of the assets (which are appraised each year). The government requires that the percentage be five percent or more.

For example, if you placed $100,000 in a charitable trust with yourself as the beneficiary drawing a six percent income interest, you would receive $6,000 in the first year of the trust's existence. If it were an annuity trust, you would get $6,000 every year until it came time to give away the trust's property. You would get $6,000 whether the remainder interest given to charity stayed at $100,000, grew to $200,000 or shrunk to $50,000. If it were a unitrust, you would get more income if the trust's value appreciated and less if it withered. Six percent of a $200,000 trust would give you a $12,000 income interest. Six percent of a $50,000 trust would give you $3,000 in income interest.

Charitable remainder trusts may be set up during the life of the individual granting the assets, or they can be created under a will. Only living charitable remainder trusts provide income tax deductions. The trust's income can go to the donor or anyone else he chooses. The remainder is given away to charity. The actuarial value of the remainder interest constitutes a deduction against income.

The econometric IRS swat teams have devised a set of tables, based on expected longevity, to determine the percentage of the fair market value of the property placed in trust which they will allow you to deduct. The older the donor, the less his life expectancy and the greater the percentage which can be deducted.

You can use the trust as a tax-saving vehicle even if you want to avoid losing the remainder interest to charity. By setting up a short term (ten year) trust, you can donate the interest to your favorite charity, get back the trust property after ten years and get a tax deduction amounting to 30 percent of the gift.

The donor stands an excellent opportunity of using an annuity trust to make a charitable contribution, reduce his taxes *and* increase his income if the appreciated property is made up of low-yield assets. If the low-yield assets are given to a trust, they can be sold tax free and invested in a more profitable medium. The new yield can then be paid to the donor, who can write off the donation from his income taxes (subject to the 30 percent rule).

Charitable remainder unitrusts pay a stipulated interest rate, whether the payment comes out of the trust's income or principal. A unitrust avoids paying capital gains on the appreciated assets it has to sell, and the income beneficiary gets to treat that portion of income as long term capital gains (which are taxed at half the usual rate).

Charity can indeed be very sweet. If you map out your options and plan your financial activity in a way to minimize taxes, charitable deductions may prove to be a lucrative loophole.

Thanksgiving Day is the time turkeys go to the chopping block. For people, it's April 15 — unless they are smart enough to chart an intelligent tax strategy a year ahead of time.

CHAPTER EIGHT

IN TRUSTS WE TRUST

"And the scribes of the Pharisees, when they saw that he was eating with sinners and tax collectors, said to his disciples, 'Why does he eat with tax collectors and sinners?"
Mark 2:16

Property rights are violated every time the legal force of government is marshalled against peaceful citizens to tax them out of their rightfully acquired income. In what is perhaps the most brashly arrogant display of illicit power and authority, government has solemnly decreed that you may not even freely give away your own possessions to your children, wife, relatives or friends.

You must strain your worldly possessions through the IRS collender before they will "allow" you the "privilege" of disposing away your property to the people you wish and in the manner you choose. If they can't tear your money away from you during your lifetime, they will suck it away while in transit between you and your heirs. You have to use *their* laws, *their* regulations and *their* rules to keep as much as possible of your rightful property beyond the clutches of the gougers in Washington. The butchers in Washington are pulling your stretched throat as far as they can, exposing it to the swift and razor-sharp blades wielded by the muggers, butchers and goons working inside the IRS slaughterhouse.

Nowhere is the travesty to justice more disproportionately ludicrous than in the rules governing the bequeathal of estates from society's most prosperous producers to those they wish to have inherit what has been built. Nowhere under the *general* subject of taxes should you be more diligent in pursuing legal remedies to retain whatever resemblence there is left remaining of property rights.

Take careful notes. Do whatever you can to make sure the Internal Revenue Service mangles, manhandles and minces you the least extent possible.

Gifts are one way to minimize the pillage. The government has written into law a provision they call the "annual exclusion". The annual exclusion presently stands at $3,000. What this means is that you can give away as much as $3,000 to any individual without paying a gift tax. A gift is a transfer of property. As such, it is *not* considered by the IRS to be income. The recipient gets a *tax-free* gift. If you go over the $3,000 annual exclusion, you are forced to pay a gift tax. The IRS requires the filing of Form 709 if your gifts in any one year — to any one person — exceed $3,000. No form need be filed if you give an individual less than $3,000. You may give less than $3,000 as a gift to as many people as you wish without paying a gift tax; neither will you have to file any notification or report with the IRS. The scoundrels have required the filing of a 709 report no later than 90 days after a gift in excess of $25,000.

One of the recent "tax reforms" combined the gift tax

with the death tax. Not only is the current tax steeply graduated, but it is cumulative as well. For example, if you give away a taxable gift of $70,000, it is taxed at the $70,000 gift rate. If you give another $30,000 taxable gift to the same person three years later, you have to pay a marginal tax rate for a $100,000 gift!

Gifts are still attractive tax vehicles due to the $3,000 annual exclusion. Title is directly granted to the heirs, probate costs and delays are eliminated and income generated by the granted gift is now produced by family members in lower tax brackets.

If the donor should die less than three years after bestowing his gift, the IRS will invoke their "three year contemplation of death rule", which states that the gift is now considered a transfer subject to the death tax. However, gifts of $3,000 may be made right up to the time of death.

It should be pointed out that most states have gift taxes which inflict even more distress on the innocent taxpayer.

Long-term irrevocable trusts have been used as legal vehicles for providing services beyond the tax savings found in gift-giving. These trusts may, for example, come in handy when it is deemed preferable to have an experienced trustee manage the money rather than simply leaving it to a possibly irresponsible recipient.

Gifts may be placed in an irrevocable trust for a minor child with the provision that should the child die, the property will be distributed among his brothers and sisters.

The money would otherwise revert back to the parents, an unfortunate result of a program that faithfully tucked away $3,000 a year into a trust dedicated to their child's future.

A rapidly expanding, closely-held family corporation is a prime candidate for a gift trust. An outright gift would exclude the present owner from enjoying the income generated by the firm. The owner of a quick-paced growth firm will face a steep, graduated death tax in years to come. An irrevocable living trust short-circuits the future tax expropriation and still provides income for the present owner.

Trusts may be set up which grant a permanent annuity income for the lifetime of the beneficiary. The value of the gift assigned to the trust is based on a fraction of the principal. The expected value of the trust is reflected by a high percentage of the principal for a younger person who is expected to live longer than an older person.

Short term irrevocable trusts set up to last a specific length of time are assigned a gift value in much the same way. The longer the trust's expected duration, the larger is the percentage of principal assigned as the value of the gift. The IRS meddlers have figured out and published sets of actuarial tables which may be used by the taxpayer to compute the deductible gift value of setting up either a trust which produces a lifetime income for a beneficiary or a short term irrevocable trust.

Most couples use wills to distribute their worldly possessions to their heirs. But trusts do a far better job. since most couples own assets in joint tenancy with the right of survival, half the assets are taxed when the first spouse dies. The entire estate is taxed when the second spouse dies. Had a marital deduction trust been used, one half the estate would have been taxed upon the first spouse's death. Not only does a trust avoid the double taxation of the first half, but the tax *rate* is lower. The estate tax schedule is steeply graduated. As such, a half-sized estate pays a much lower tax rate and pays far *less* than half the tax levy that would befall an estate twice its size. Marital deduction trusts leave half the joint estate to the living spouse in trust for the children. It is not taxed again. It has the same tax effect as leaving half the joint estate directly to the children, plus it has a couple of extra advantages.

All income from the entrusted half can go to the surviving spouse. What's more, the spouse can take $5,000 each year out of the trust's principal (or 5 percent each year, whichever is greater). A marital deduction trust does not impose any extra estate tax burden on the property; it gives financial security to the surviving spouse, and, if named trustee, the surviving partner can even maintain complete control of the property.

There are three basic marital deduction rules which must be met to set up a marital deduction trust. The surviving spouse must first be given a life-time entitlement to all income produced off the property. The income must be paid to the spouse at least once a year. The surviving spouse must be free to give away her half of the estate to whomever she pleases.

When the children of the estate owner are fairly well-to-do, the bestowal of additional assets will expand an income that is already heavily pelted by taxes. One solution is to leave the estate to the young grandchildren. This financial technique, known as "generation skipping", can drastically reduce taxes. If the estate holder, his children and his grandchildren are each sliced by a 30 percent death tax, a one million dollar estate is devastated to $343,000! In some instances up to $250,000 of property can be transferred tax free through a generation skipping trust.

The estate may directly be given away to the grandchildren; but if the estate owner does not wish to bypass his children, he may set up a trust for his grandchildren and give the trust's income to his grandchildren, meaning his grandchildren may decide who shall inherit the estate's assets. The power of appointment enables the estate to skip *two* generations.

The rule against perpetuity was devised to stop a trust from continuing indefinitely. It requires that the heirs must be alive at the time the trust was created. No trust can last longer than two lifetimes in being plus 21 years.

Trusts may be used to reduce overall family income taxes by shifting income from high tax bracket family members to low bracket members.

A trust is a separate tax paying entity. An individual in a high tax bracket can put property in a trust where, due to the painfully graduated income tax, accumulated income will be shredded less severely by government. If trust income can be distributed to children who earn less than $750 a year, neither the trust nor the child nor the high tax bracket individual will pay any taxes whatsoever.

Two trusts of interest to those who want to use trusts as vehicles for reducing income taxes are the irrevocable living trust and the revocable testamentary trust.

Irrevocable living trusts are used to spread income among family members and thereby reduce income taxes. Short term trusts must last longer than ten years. Long term trusts may last the life of the testator. The money reverts back to the testator upon the trust's expiration. Whether the trust's income goes to the children or simply accumulates in the trust, income tax savings are made. The IRS will not permit the establishment of a short term irrevocable trust if the beneficiary has a life expectancy of less than ten years.

Testamentary trusts, created by will, are helpful in the establishment of family trusts, which circumvent the problem of setting up separate trusts for each child. The trustee is empowered with discretion in disposal of the fund's income among the recipients.

The power of appointment gives another person the power of decision over who shall receive the income and principal of the estate. A husband may give the power of appointment to his wife, for example, with the purpose in mind of giving her a chance to consider the financial shape of her children before disposing of the trust's assets.

"But the tax collector, standing far off, would not even lift up his eyes to heaven, but beat his breast, saying, "God, be merciful to me a sinner!"

Luke 18:13

PART III

AX THE TAX

"Government is a broker in pillage, and every election is a sort of advance auction sale in stolen goods."
H. L. Menchen

CHAPTER NINE

INVESTMENT SHIELDS

"When the tax burden grows beyond a bearable size, the problem of devising taxes that will not discourage and disrupt production becomes insoluble."

Henry Hazlitt

If anything at all can be gleaned from the pages of history, it is the repeated failure of a country to survive once it imposes a tax burden on its citizens exceeding a third of their earnings. Disintegration sets in at 25 percent. Things are falling apart today in large part because of the 48 percent excoriation the American taxpayer receives from the hands of the tax collectors, politicians and bureaucrats. Were it not for special investment incentives such as loopholes and tax shelters, no one would have any incentive whatever to produce anything in modern-day America.

Abraham Lincoln once said the best way to get a bad law repealed is to enforce it strictly. It is obvious that the politicians are using investment loopholes as inferior substitutes for general tax reductions. The tax law is slowly choking our economy to death. Until genuine tax relief comes, the only way you can keep yourself financially alive is to climb through every single opening in the massive tax wall. The wall is blocking productivity and stopping all economic process. Every time you slip through, you are doing a favor for yourself, for your family and for economic progress.

From the point of view of individual tax relief, Wall Street offers a number of attractive possibilities. Primary consideration lies in the long term capital gains tax, which taxes only half the profit made on appreciated property held for longer than a year.

The tax mechanics on Schedule D of the onerous 1040 form require the investor to separately list and balance both long and short term capital gains against long and short term capital losses.

A cumulative short term capital gain is taxed like any other income. A net short term loss is deducted like any other deduction. A cumulative long term gain is divided in half before being added to taxable income. Likewise, only half of a long term loss is deductible, up to $3,000 in a single year. The remainder can be used up by carrying it forward to future years.

The predators in Washington have disallowed any loss on a stock when the same security is bought within 30 days before or after the sale. But the incremental loss is added to the cost basis of the new security.

All short sales are decreed by the IRS to be short term in nature.

It is important to designate specifically which shares you sell. If you bought share number 3827 two years ago and share number 8872 last week, you must sell share 3827 to get a long term capital gain.

Appreciated property *is not* subject to *any* capital gains tax when it is passed along to heirs in an estate. The value of the property becomes the heir's new cost basis. Don't suffer, however, from the illusion that the property is not fired upon because the IRS carves away a portion with assistance from the death tax. Under the 1976 tax revisions this law is changing, and in the future, capital gains will be subject to income tax, as well as the asset being taxed as part of the estate.

The first $100 you get from dividends is tax deductible, and you get a $200 dividend exclusion on joint returns. The rest is taxed as regular income. It should be pointed out that dividend income is actually bludgeoned twice. The IRS grazes some away through the corporate income tax before you receive your dividend check. Some of your dividend income is then cropped away.

Stock dividends are distributions of stock and not considered income until sold. They are not taxable. Neither are stock splits because they merely multiply the number of shares you and everybody else has over a fixed amount of assets.

The IRS scalawags will *not* let you deduct such investment-related expenses as legal fees, safety deposit box fees for tax-free bonds or brokerage commissions! Instead, commissions are incorporated into the cost basis of the stock. They are added when you buy and subtracted when you sell.

The thieves in Washington cannot lay a hand on even

one cent of the interest you earn off municipal bonds. Many people believe that since 96 percent of the tax-free municipal bonds are owned by 7½ percent of the wealthiest people in America that these bonds are exclusively used by rich people.

Incomes that are 70 percent ensnared by the IRS plunderers must earn 23.33 percent on their money to keep 7 percent for themselves. Clearly, a 7 percent tax exempt income from a municipal bond is as attractive to such people as a 23.33 percent taxable income from a corporate bond. Actually, the 7 percent tax-free bond is *more* attractive because a bond which yields 23.33 percent is probably very risky. A 7 percent tax-exempt municipal bond equates to the yield off a 14 percent taxable bond for people in the 50 percent tax bracket.

It should be obvious that even people of moderate means can benefit from buying municipal bonds. A tax-free 7 percent is equivalent to a taxable 9.33 percent yield to the individual in the 25 percent tax bracket! Municipal bond income is exempt from state income taxes, too.

Forty-three states impose a state income tax. The **total** tax bracket should be considered when comparing taxable and tax-exempt yields. For example, a New Yorker in the 70 percent federal tax bracket is also in the 15 percent state tax bracket. He ordinarily surrenders 85 percent of his income to the authorities, which means a 7 percent municipal bond yield converts to the **46.67 percent** yield he would have to get from a taxable debenture.

The single Californian earning $30,000 a year must get

more than a 15.9 percent taxable yield to equal the tax-free yield off a 7 percent municipal bond.

Several points should be considered before putting your money into a municipal bond. First and foremost, you had better make sure the state, county, city or authority is reasonably solvent. Most municipal bonds are pretty solid. Only two percent of the municipal bonds defaulted at the depth of the Great Depression, and even the defaulted bonds paid off in full at maturity. You should look at the issuing authority's debt history. This is their credit rating. It better be good. You should lower your rating if there are plans for a mass transit system. Such programs are usually losers that must be heavily subsidized.

The local economy's industrial base should be broad -- not reliant on a few industries. A narrow base exposes the locality to the risk of a move or economic slowdown that could seriously impact the ability to pay the bond's interest. Avoid areas with stable or declining populations. Regions with growing populations are more healthy and dynamic. They promise a more solid tax base.

Real estate is another field rich in tax-saving strategies. The property owner can deduct property taxes, mortgage interest and depreciation if the property is not his home. If sold after a year, the profit is taxed as a long term capital gain.

Depreciation can artificially lower the income tax of property. Many times depreciation will enable you to report a tax loss even if you really make money. Of course,

76

depreciation merely defers the tax. It doesn't get rid of it. But in reducing current income and making it taxable upon sale of the property, ordinary income (which is taxed at ordinary rates) is translated into a long term capital gain and pays a lower tax rate.

The tax advantages are amplified when making a low down payment. As little as 25 percent can be put down on investment property. As little as five or ten percent can be applied toward the down payment of a home. In both cases, a thin initial equity magnifies the percentage of profit as the property increases in value. Business property is depreciated on the entire cost of the building, meaning a large tax deduction can be taken against equity.

Taxes can be deferred more quickly through the use of non-straight line (accelerated) depreciation. Two well-used methods are the declining balance method and the sum of the year's digits method. Both are explained in any introductory accounting book or in Money Book No. 1 of this series..

Congress has launched an attack against accelerated depreciation. As might be expected, the depreciation schedule chart (with the noted exception of straight line depreciation) is now very complicated.

When you buy new residential property, you can still use either the 200 percent declining balance method or the sum of the years digits technique. New non-residential property bought after July 24, 1969, can use the 125 percent declining balance method provided it has an expected life of 20 or more years.

Depreciation is taken at the fastest pace with apartments, hotels and theatres, which have a straight line depreciation of 2½ percent a year. Office buildings, factories, farm buildings, garages and machine shops have been decreed to have useful lives of 45 years. Hence, their straight line depreciation rate falls to an annual 2.22 percent. Houses, stores, loft buildings and banks are permitted a 2 percent straight line depreciation. Warehouses and elevators have a stipulated 1.67 percent depreciation.

The IRS has assigned a three year useful life to a car (33.3 percent), a four year useful life to light general purpose trucks (25 percent) and a six year life to planes and heavy general purpose trucks (16.67 percent).

Property taxes and interest paid on construction loans are deductible for the person constructing a new building -- even though there is no income against which it could be taken.

There are even steps that may be taken to avoid the capital gains tax! No capital gains tax is slapped on the exchange of property if the property you both give and receive is of a business nature.

If you are older than 65 and your home has been your principal residence, you can escape paying a large part of the capital gains tax. Divide the sales price of your home into $20,000 and multiply that figure by the amount of your capital gains. This dollar figure is the amount you can exclude from the capital gains subject to tax. If, for example, you had bought a home for $60,000 and sold it for $110,000, you would have $50,000 in capital gains. Dividing that figure into $20,000 produces the number 4. When you multiply .4 by $50,000, you arrive at $20,000, which means you have a long term capital gain of $30,000 -- only half of which is taxable.

Nor do you have to pay a capital gains tax on your home if you invest all the proceeds from the sale into a new home. Capital gains taxes are avoided by giving away your property. As said earlier, the tax is bypassed when leaving appreciated property to your heirs -- but it's still zapped by the death tax.

Installment sales contracts can be used as another way of reducing the capital gains tax by deferring it to a later time when it will be taxed at a lower rate. The seller can receive no more than 30 percent of the selling price in the first year of the property sale if he wishes to qualify for the tax break in the installment sales contract.

Gross profit is divided by the contract price to determine the portion of each year's installment payment which con stitutes long term capital gain.

Mutual funds are to the stock market what REITs are to real estate. REIT is the acronym for "Real Estate Investment Trust". REIT's enable people to pool their money together and buy pieces of property they otherwise couldn't afford to buy. REITs are conduits through which real estate income passes. As such, they are not subject to any income tax. To qualify as a REIT, the trust must get 90 percent of its gross income from rent, interest, property tax refunds and the gains from selling property and securities. Seventy-five percent or more of its gross income must come from real estate. Less than 30 percent of its income should come from short term stock sales and sales of real estate held for less than four years.

One last real estate loophole is the use of a part of your home as office space. A bona fide office enables you to deduct a pro rata share of the home's depreciation and maintenance costs. It is important that you be able to prove the portion of your home space the office occupies, how much you use it, what purpose the office was used for and that the space was an actual necessity to perform your job.

You can place your money beyond the reach of the tax crooks in Washington by investing in a venture involved with an extraction process.

Over one hundred industries have been granted depletion allowances. In addition to oil and natural gas, depletion allowances exist for timber, sulphur, iron ore, sand and gravel, oyster and clam shells, ball and sogger clay, flower pot clay and limestone. The depletion allowance is as high as 22 percent on oil, gas, sulphur and uranium, asbestos, lead, zinc and nickel. It is as low as 5 percent for sand and gravel. Gold, silver, oil shale, copper and iron ore enjoy a 15 percent depletion allowance. Coal and sulphur chloride get 10 percent. Most minerals get 14 percent.

While normal cost depletion divides the cost of the property less the cost of the land by the number of recoverable units, the percentage depletion excludes a set percentage of the gross income from taxes. The IRS henchmen have set a depletion allowance limitation of 50 percent of the net taxable income. With a 15 percent depletion allowance and a gross income of $1,000,000, the investor can completely exclude $150,000 from his taxes. What's more, he can do this every year, long past the time the original investment cost has been recaptured.

The whole cost can be deducted if you sink a dry well. You can also depreciate tangible property like pipes, casing, tubing and machines. Roughly 80 percent of intangible drilling expenses can be deducted the first year. This includes fuel, hauling, wages and incidental supply costs.

Drilling for oil is no easy venture. Only one out of every ten wildcat wells hits oil. An exploratory well costs $200,000. You should have enough money to drill 50 wells -- which means you must have ten million dollars.

Limited partnerships have enabled investors to pool their money, get around this capital problem and reduce risks significantly. While a single wildcat well stands a mere 10 percent chance of striking oil, your odds in a limited partnership, prepared to sink 50 wells, rises to 99½ percent.

Timber is the largest benefactor from depletion allowances, next to oil and gas. Since a timber crop takes 40 to 50 years to grow, the profit from timber is taxed as a capital gain. Half is excluded from taxes. If a loss is incurred, the IRS lets you deduct the **full loss!** Before you pack your bags and head for the timber line, take out your umbrella and consider tax shelters as yet another way to keep your property from winding up as booty inside the IRS warchest.

Tax shelters are financial devices which enable a taxpayer to shower his income with artificial losses from what appear at first glance to be unprofitable undertakings. A tax shelter writes these losses off as deductions against current income. An example already given of a tax shelter was the tax and interest expense in constructing a new building. Such costs precede rental income. Instead of deducting these costs against this future rental income, you can make a deduction against **current** income!

In addition to real estate construction costs, other tax shelters can be found in accelerated depreciation in excess of straight line, intangible oil and gas drilling costs, capital gains, cattle feeding, vineyards and orchards. Cattle feeding, vineyards and orchard investments have been determined by the Internal Revenue Service to be activities classified as "farming for a profit". In such cases, the case method of accounting is permitted. The cattle feeder can deduct interest expenses, feeding expenses and prepaid feeding expenses. He can bring his deductible prepaid expenses as high as 200 percent, and while the oil well drills, can easily pull out any time he likes.

Vineyard and orchard investors can expense the three or four year wait for their shrubs to mature. Labor, fertilizer, tax and other costs can be written off against today's current income, years before the first piece of fruit is picked.

"The will of man is not shattered but softly bent and guided; men are seldom forced to act, but they are constantly restrained from acting; such a power does not destroy, but it prevents existence; it does not tyrannize, but it compresses, enervates, extinguishes and stupefies a people, till each nation is reduced to be nothing better than a flock of timid and industrious animals, of which government is the shepherd."

Alex De Toqueville

CHAPTER TEN

BASIC TAX STRATEGIES

"I'm trying to avoid payment of taxes this year by declaring New York City as a dependent."

Johnny Carson

By filing forms 4868 and 7004, you can delay paying your taxes by extending the deadline two months past the normal date for filing the return. You can get another six months extension if you provide a good reason, but you must pay the taxes you believe will be chomped off by the IRS racketeers.

If you have a corporation and pay the first tax installment on or before the due date, you can receive an automatic three month extension.

Two kinds of government savings bonds offer a way to get around the tax bombardment. "E" bonds grow in value. "H" bonds pay current interest through two semi-annual checks. Interest on these bonds is not taxed until collected. A retiring citizen holding a cache of "E" bonds can defer taxes by converting them to money in small quantities during the autumn of his life, when both income and income taxes are low. Or he can convert them to "H" bonds with the deferred interest stamped on the bond. It will be taxed when converted into money.

No one has to pay more than 25 percent on long term capital gains less than $50,000 in a single year. If you make more than $50,000 in long term capital gains, you can use the alternate tax on capital gains. The first $50,000 is taxed at 25 percent and the remainder is taxed at the individual's tax bracket. The alternate tax can be used whether or not you earn more than $50,000 in capital gains. It is a good idea to compare the taxes you would owe under both the usual capital gains treatment and the alternate treatment. Use the one that results in fewer taxes.

The IRS has given another "break" to us in the form of a maximum tax on what they condescendingly refer to as "earned" income (wages, salaries, tips, fees, bonuses, commissions, tips, prizes and awards). Under the maximum tax, no one is dehydrated by more than half his "earned" income, regardless of his tax bracket. The marauders don't look at total taxable income to determine this maximum tax. Rather, the "earned" taxable income is the governing factor.

You break the 50 percent marginal tax level if you are single with an earned taxable income over $40,200; if you are married with a joint taxable income over $55,200; if you are married with a separate filed return reporting an income over $27,600; or if you are an unmarried household head earning more than $40,200.

85

Three computations are involved with figuring out the joint tax. You are required to first pay whatever tax the rate schedules mandate up to the 50 percent marginal breaking point. You then subtract your total earned taxable income from the income level where the marginal tax rate is 50 percent ($40,200, $55,200 or $27,600, depending on your filing status). Your tax rate on this income is 50 percent. Add the two taxes together. You'll never have to hand over more than half your earned income to the tax collectors in Washington, D. C. But you *will* have to wade through the banter, drivel and palaver on special IRS form 4726.

If your income substantially increases in any one year, you may income average. You must have an averageable income that is greater than $3,000 to use this technique. Averageable income is the amount by which the taxpayer's adjusted taxable income in his boom year is greater than 30 percent of his TOTAL TAXABLE INCOME for the last four years (referred to as the base period years).

If your boom year income is $3,000 greater than 30 percent of your base period years, you may income average. To do this, you file Schedule G. The taxpayer first computes 30 percent of his combined base period income. He figures out the tax on this amount. He then takes one-fifth of his averageable income, figures out the tax, multiplies the tax by five and adds this to the tax on 30 percent of his base period income. This is the tax he owes.

If income averaging is used, the taxpayer cannot take tax advantage of the alternate tax on capital gains, the exclusion of foreign income or the maximum tax on earned income.

Unemployment insurance, scholarships, fellowships and life, casualty, accident and health insurance proceeds may be entirely excluded from your income which is subject to tax.

ANNUITIES

An annuity is a contract which guarantees to pay you an income at some future date (the settlement date). The contract guarantees the interest you will earn during the accummulation period prior to that settlement date and guarantees the income you would be paid under the various payment options the contract provides. In most cases today the amount of interest actually being paid on the accummulations is substantially higher than the guaranteed rate. Most annuities today guarantee 4%, but many are actually paying interest from 7½ to 8¾%. Since these earnings are tax deferred, the compound earnings are very substantial over 20 or 30 years.

Most annuities are underwritten and issued by life insurance companies throughout the United States. They are closely regulated and subject to the regulations of each insurance department in every state in which they conduct business.

Under the terms of the internal revenue code, no income tax is payable on an annuity until annuity income payments commence. Even then, further tax advantages are available. This means, for you, that your capital in the annuity grows "tax free" until you withdraw more than you have paid in or begin to receive periodic payments.

Income Tax Advantages at Retirement

There are several income tax advantages at retirement. First, when you become 65 you will be entitled to two deductions. This will directly reduce the amount of your income that will be subject to tax. Second, once you do retire, your income will probably decrease, putting you in a lower bracket. These advantages, of course, are available to anyone who reaches 65 and retires.

There are some special advantages to annuity income, however, that are not available to any of your other investment income. Under the Tax Reform Act 1976, the classification of annuity income has been changed so that in the future it will be considered to be part of 'personal service taxable income' and not taxable at a rate of more than 50%.

There is one final advantage; an annuity is designed to make payments to you for as long as you live — however long that may be. Thus, each payment is an actuarially calculated combination of principal and interest. When you first start to take annuity payments, a calculation is made based on your probable life expectancy which will result in some part of each annuity payment that you receive being income tax free. Thereafter, the same portion of each payment will be tax free no matter how much you have received or how long payments are made to you.

All annuity contracts provide certain guarantees. They

guarantee the safety of principal, for one thing, and that a given income will be paid at retirement (though they can't guarantee the purchasing power of the dollar at that time). For instance, an annuity may guarantee to pay a male, age 65, $7.02 per $1,000 accumulated in the contract, but currently be paying $8.64 per $1,000 — for life. Annuities also guarantee a minimum interest rate during the accumulation period (like 4%) but, as stated above, they may actually be crediting 7 or 8 or 9%, depending on interest rates and money markets at the time.

Annuities are always designed for a long period of accumulation — 10 or 20 years or more. With long range results being of the greatest importance, the company issuing the annuity invests its money in long term assets. If an annuity is surrendered before its term has expired, then the company must sell shorter term investments to provide the cash to pay the surrender value. This involves considerable cost due to fees and additional work and means that the short run return for the annuity is less. Usually, these costs are combined and one rate is supplied which applies in any event.

Income from an annuity is calculated at the time that you decide to begin to receive payments. The calculation is a simple one — the current rate per thousand is multiplied by the number of thousands in your contract and that is your income. The option frequently used is called the ten year certain life option. This means that you, or your beneficiary, will receive an income for ten years; the same income would be paid to you for as long as you live.

An annuity payment is an actuarial blend of interest and principal with the calculation made to assure that you cannot outlast the income. Once annuity payments to you start, the same payment will be made to you each month as long as you live. Since there is a blending of income and principal, you are not taxed on the return of the principal. Assuming payments to you will last more than three years, a calculation is made, when payments to you start, as to how much of each payment is taxable. Thereafter, however long payments to you continue, the same portion of each payment is tax free.

You have many income options to choose among:
. . . an income for your life, however long that may be
. . . an income guaranteed for some period (or amount) and for your life thereafter
. . . Installment payments in a specified amount
. . . Installment payments for a specified period
. . . a joint and survivor annuity payable for the life of you and your beneficiary

You are not required to begin taking payments at 65. You may begin earlier, or later, and in some cases you may defer commencement of payment to age 85.

An annuity may be purchased by a single premium payment or accumulated over a period of time by a series of premium payments. You may own the annuity yourself or have another person designated as owner. You may buy an annuity on another person's life, if that person agrees, and own it, with payments, when made, coming to you.

QUALIFIED TAX DEFERRED KEOGH PLANS AND INDIVIDUAL RETIREMENT ANNUITIES

The Keogh Plan offers a way for the self-employed to defer income taxes. You may deduct 15 percent of your "earned" income under this plan, up to a limit of $7,500. The investment vehicle chosen for you may be a bank, an insurance company, a mutual fund or some other institution "authorized" by the law. What you set aside in a Keogh Plan is not taxed by the government. Neither is the interest. The man who puts aside $7,500 a year for 20 years defers taxes on $150,000, and, at 6 percent, accumulates a *$276,000* nest egg. At 10 percent, the sum grows to $430,000.

A $7,500 Keogh Plan deposit may be deducted against your taxable income. That means a *tax savings* of $3,000 if you are in the 40 percent tax bracket.

The government won't let you tap into your Keogh account until you pass the age of 59½. They level substantial penalties on you if you do. Keogh is a great way to defer paying high taxes on some of the money you earn in your peak producing years. You only pay taxes on the amount you withdraw.

But Keogh is not all peaches and cream. In addition to substantial penalties on pre-schedule withdrawals, your Keogh holdings are exposed to the ravishes of inflation. With a six percent inflation rate, a six percent gross yield translates into zero gain. A ten percent annual gross yield translates into a four percent net yield. The investor's profit is slashed by almost 74 percent.

If you start contributing toward a Keogh Plan, you must be self-employed, and you may not be covered by a company pension plan. You will have to set up Keogh accounts for your fulltime employees who have worked for you longer than three years, and this will require you to make contributions into their retirements funds.

You may set up an Individual Retirement Account (IRA) even if you are not self-employed. In a manner similar to Keogh, you may deduct up to 15 percent of your "earned" income, to a maximum of $1,500, or $1,750 if the wife is not employed. A husband-wife team can contribute up to $3,000 a year if both of them work, and meet the government's "eligibility requirements".

Another tax angle which can effectively be used is the corporation. In addition to the advantages of limited liability, the corporation can be used as a tool to lower tax rates. After meeting all expenses, including the salaries of managers and officers, the corporation only pays 20 percent on the first $25,000 of taxable profits. A marginal 22 percent tax is slapped on the next $25,000 earned. A 48 percent tax ceiling is placed on taxable profits exceeding $50,000.

A subchapter "S" corporation may be used to avoid the double corporate-personal tax altogether. To qualify, it must have ten or fewer shareholders and the decision to elect chapter "S" standing must be unanimous. The corporate profit or loss is distributed each year to the shareholders. Since some states throw a state income tax on subchapter "S" corporations, it may be advisable to distribute pro-rata salaries to shareholders equal to an amount that exhausts the pool of profits. Subchapter "S" corporations are especially valuable during the early years of the firm, when losses are expected to occur.

Under a corporation pension and/or profit sharing program, plans can be set up which may allow substantially larger tax free deductions than a Keogh or IRA account. Many businessmen incorporate for this very reason — to put aside larger amounts for their retirement on a tax deferred basis.

Incorporation procedures are quick, simple, easy and inexpensive. A book published by Ted Nicholas outlines the steps you can take to charter your own corporation yourself, for less than 50 dollars. Included for your convenience are easy-to-complete, ready-made forms.

Taxpayers in search of a refuge could very well find a welcome institutional framework in the corporation. Over 25,000 corporations come into being every month. There are over 1.7 million corporations presently operating in America! Ted Nicholas highly recommends the use of Delaware as a corporate domicile. The taxes are low, the service fast, the requirements simple and the business atmosphere receptive. There is even a special Delaware court system for the corporations known as the Court of Chancery. Delaware is the home of 38 percent of the corporations listed on the New York Stock Exchange. With only 3/10 of one percent of America's population living within the borders of the state, its pro rata share of corporations comes down a hefty 141 times. The closest runner-up is Maryland, whos pro-rate share is a meager 1.6! Delaware's pro-rata share of corporation homes is 89 times larger than New York, the second major incorporation state.

Small corporations may opt for special tax insurance under the Small Business Section 1244 Election. In the event of business failure, $25,000 of capital losses may be deducted each year ($50,000 for a joint return). Normally, you would be limited to a $3,000 deduction with the balance taking the form of a carryforward.

If you expect your present year's income to be greater than next year's, it is advisable to delay your income such that it is earned at a lower tax rate. One way to do this near year end is to delay title transfer of goods until a specific future date. This may be done by imposing the restriction that the sale is finalized upon fulfillment of a condition that will materialize in a timely manner. One method is to tie completion of the sale to the installation of goods that are actually in the process of working in the productive process.

Deductions should be accelerated in years of high income. Bad debts can be written off. So can damaged or obsolete inventory. Keogh deductions can be increased to the 15 percent limit. Employee bonuses can be distributed earlier. Early equipment repairs and prepayments of valid business expenses serve to speed up deductions.

Prepayments may be expensed for advertising, rent, subscriptions, dues, insurance premiums and countless other items.

One final domestic tax strategy comes in the area of maximizing after tax yield on a stock. A security must be held longer than a year to receive the benefit of capital gains treatment. A problem surfaces for the investor who believes his stock is going to fall when it has a few months left to wait until his short term profit transforms itself into a long term gain. The problem translates into the question of how much the stock will drop before the lower long term capital gains are worth less than the high short term capital gains.

The investor checks the marginal tax rate he paid last year and divides it by 100. He first subtracts the number from one and sets the new number aside as the numerator of a fraction. He then divides his marginal tax rate for last year by 200 and subtracts it from one. The product is set aside as the denominator of a fraction.

The numerator is divided into the denominator. The resulting number is subtracted from 1. Now, multiply the resulting figure by 100. This is the percentage the stock's capital gain must fall before a short term capital gain is preferable to a long term capital gain.

Suppose your last year's marginal tax rate was 32 percent. The numerator becomes 1-.32 or .68. The denominator becomes 1-.16 or .84. The ratio of the two is .8095. Subtracted from 1 gives .1905. Multipled by 100 gives

19.05. Rounding the number gives 19. A stock's long term profit must fall 19 percent before a person in the 32 percent tax bracket should sell for a short term gain.

If such an individual had bought a stock at 30 and had watched it rise to 45 in less than a year, he would have a $15 profit, 19 percent of which is $2.85 or (2 7/8 points per share). It would be wise for him to hold the stock more than a year if it fell no lower than 42⅛.

Tax havens sprinkled throughout the globe offer one last remaining option to the weary American taxpayer. Antigua, the Bahamas, Barbados, the Cayman Islands, the Channel Islands, Gibralter, Hong Kong, Liberia, New Hebrides, the Turks and Caicos Islands are all options the tax bitter taxpayer might consider. More detailed information can be acquired by writing to the Enterprise Publishing Company at 1300 Market Street in Wilmington, Delaware, 19801.

"I'm proud to be paying taxes in the United States. The only thing is — I could be just as proud for half the money."
Arthur Godfrey

TAX QUOTES

Taxation is the economic rape of the productive citizen. You can either relax and try to enjoy it; or you can galvanize your spirits with fortitude, and challenge the merciless edicts of the IRS with defiant tenacity and courage. To help motivate you along the path of tax freedom come the following insightful and sagacious pearls of wisdom from the wise men, sages, and pundits of our age in answer to the fool, folly, and fumble-ism so abundantly found in our nation's capitol.

"Lord, the money we do spend on government, and it's not one bit better than the government we got for one-third the money twenty years ago."

Will Rogers

Members of Congress dispose of one large tax bill after another. That's the advantage of being a congressman. The rest of us have to pay ours."

Fletcher Knebel

"The power to tax is the power to destroy."

Lord Acton

"Now the tax collectors and sinners were all drawing near to him. And the Pharisees and the scribes murmured, saying, "This man receives sinners and eats with them."

Luke 15:1

"Many find it easier to believe in the Abominable Snowman than in a creature who is supposed to pay his taxes voluntarily and in full."

Business Week

"To compel a man to furnish contributions of money for the propagation of options which he disbelieves is sinful and tyrannical."

Thomas Jefferson

"The sixteenth Amendment will of necessity have inquisitorial features; it will provide penalties. It will create a complicated machinery . . . . . business will be hauled into distant courts. Many fines will constantly menace the taxpayer. An army of federal inspectors, spies, and detectives will descend upon the state. They will compel men of business to show their books and disclose their secrets. They will require statements and affidavits. The inspector can blackmail the taxpayer."

Richard E. Byrd, March 5, 1910

"The accumulation of all powers, legislative, executive, and judiciary, in the same hands, whether in one, a few, and whether hereditary, appointed, or elective, may justly be pronounced the very definition of tyranny."

James Madison
The Federalist, No. 47

"No man's life, liberty, or property are safe while the legislature is in session."

Judge Tucker

"In questions of power, then, let no more be heard of confidence in man, but let us bind him down from mischief by the chains of the constitution."

Thomas Jefferson

"I doubt that there is a person in the United States who couldn't be convicted of a technical violation of some aspect of the personal income tax laws."

Milton Friedman

"Government is not reason, it is not eloquence; it is force. Like fire, it is both a dangerous servant and a fearful master."

George Washington

"The control of the production of wealth is the control of human life itself."

Hilaire Belloc

"Government has taken on a vast mass of new duties and responsibilities; it has spread out its powers until they penetrate to every act of the citizen, however secret; it has begun to throw around its operations the high dignity and impeccability of a religion; its agents become a separate and superior caste, with authority to bind and loose, and their thumbs in every pot. But it still remains, as it was in the beginning, the common enemy of all well-disposed, industrious, and decent men."

H.L. Mencken

"Our forefathers made one mistake. What they should have fought for was representation without taxation."

Fletcher Knebel

"A single instance in which a plainly written provision of the Constitution has been denied might in a moral point of view, justify revolution — it certainly would if such a right were a vital one."

Abraham Lincoln

"Who does not obey shall not eat."

Leon Trotsky

"Highly graduated taxation realizes most completely the supreme danger of democracy, creating a state of things in which one class imposes on another burdens which it is not asked to share, and impels the state into vast schemes of extravagance, under the belief that the whole cost will be thrown upon others."

W.E. Lecky

"Sometimes the law defends plunder and participates in it. Thus the beneficiaries are spared the shame, danger, and scruple which their acts would otherwise involve. Sometimes the law places the whole apparatus of judges, police, prisons, and gendarmes at the service of the plunderers, and treats the victim — when he defends himself — as a criminal."

Frederic Bastiat

"Government is the only agency that can take a useful commodity, like paper, slap some ink on it, and make it totally worthless."

Ludwig von Mises

"No men living are more worthy to be trusted than those who toil up from poverty, none less inclined to take or touch aught which they have not honestly earned. Let them beware of surrendering a political power which they already possess, and which, if surrendered, will surely be used to close the door of advancement against such as they, and to fix new disabilities and burdens upon them, till all of liberty shall be lost."

Abraham Lincoln

"There is something wrong with any law that causes many people to have to take a whole day off their jobs just to find out how to comply."

T. Coleman Andrews
Former IRS Director

"And there was a man named Zacchaeus; he was a chief tax collector, and rich."

Luke 19:2

"We don't want to let a nickel due us get away."
Dana Latham,
Former IRS Commissioner

1980-81 SUPPLEMENT

Fifty More Tax Savings Ideas

INDEX

SURVIVING SPOUSE CAN USE JOINT RETURN RATES

A surviving spouse (widow or widower), providing certain requirements are met, may continue to use the joint return tax rates for two taxable years following the death of the husband or wife. For the calendar year 1979, therefore, a widow or widower qualifies for the joint return rate if the spouse died any time during 1977 or 1978. Since the joint return rates are more generous than either head of household or single rates, the tax savings can be significant.

To qualify for this special treatment, there are several requirements that must be met:

- The surviving spouse must not remarry before the close of the taxable year.

- The benefit is afforded the survivor only if he or she was entitled to file a joint return with the spouse during the latter's lifetime.

- During the year of filing, the surviving spouse must provide a home which is the principal residence for the entire year of a son, daughter, stepson or stepdaughter. Furthermore, this child must qualify as a dependent for tax purposes. The joint return option is lost if the child moves out before the end of the tax year or fails to qualify as a dependent.

It must be understood that the special benefit entitles the survivor only to the joint return tax rates. It does not allow for the filing of a joint return nor does it allow any special exemptions beyond the survivor and his or her dependents.

"WASH SALE" RULES
Wait 31 Days To Rebuy Stock Sold For Loss

Many unsuspecting investors lose a tax deduction for a loss on the sale of stocks or other securities because they are unfamiliar with the "wash sale" rules. Specifically, the "wash sale" prohibits recognizing the loss on the sale of stocks or other securities in cases where "substantially identical" securities are acquired within 30 days before or after the sale. Therefore, if you sell a stock for a loss, you must wait 31 days from the date of the transaction to rebuy the stock. Alternately, if you had utilized the so-called doubling up technique and bought an equal number of shares of the security to be sold for a loss, the original shares could not be sold until the 31-day period expired.

The "wash sale" does not apply when the securities are sold for a profit. Neither does it apply if similar but not identical securities are purchased within the 31-day period. For example, you could sell General Motors for a loss and buy Ford immediately with no adverse tax consequences.

One other important point to remember is that even if a loss is disallowed because of the "wash sale," the cost basis for the newly acquired shares can be adjusted by the amount of the loss. Therefore, when you eventually sell the new holding, the disallowed loss will decrease your profit or increase your loss. In effect, the "wash sale" delayed but did not permanently eliminate your tax deduction.

THE ORPHAN'S EXCLUSION
Estate Tax Deduction For Orphaned Children

A little known provision of the 1976 Tax Reform Act is the "orphan's exclusion." Specifically, it provides for a new estate tax deduction for children orphaned before age 21. To qualify, the child must be under 21 at the time of the decedent's death and have no surviving parent (or no surviving spouse of the decedent). The maximum estate tax deduction is $5,000 for each year the child is under age 21.

Since many parents are reluctant to leave assets outright to minor children, the "orphan's exclusion" can be used in conjunction with a properly created trust. Furthermore, the deduction will not be lost even if the property in the trust will pass to a third party should the child die before reaching age 21.

INVOLUNTARY CONVERSION
Defer Capital Gain On Destroyed Property

Inflationary pressures over the past decade have pushed real estate values to dizzying heights. This in turn means that today, most property is insured for substantially more than its original cost. This introduces the possibility that if the property is destroyed, the insurance proceeds will yield a substantial capital gain. Is such an unintentional gain subject to capital gains tax? The answer is not necessarily.

According to current tax statutes, no gain is recognized if property, as a result of its destruction, theft, seizure, requisition or condemnation, is involuntarily converted into replacement property which has an equal or greater value. To the extent that the proceeds from an involuntary conversion are not invested in replacement property, the gain is recognized in the year in which it is received.

105

To qualify as replacement property, according to IRS rules, it must be similar or related in service or use to the property destroyed. Alternately, instead of acquiring a similar piece of property, it is acceptable to buy controlling interest (at least 80%) of a corporation which owns property that is similar or related in service or use. An actual purchase must take place. An enforceable contract to purchase is not sufficient.

The replacement property, or controlling interest in a corporation which owns such property, must be acquired within two years after the close of the first taxable year in which any part of the gain resulting from the involuntary conversion is realized.

IRA ROLLOVER
Defer Tax Liability On Lump Sum Pension Distribution

Those not covered by an approved tax-sheltered retirement or profit-sharing program can create their own tax-free pension plan (an Individual Retirement Account). Up to 15% of gross income, to a maximum of $1,500, can be set aside each year. If a joint account is set up between husband and wife and one of the spouses is not employed, the maximum is raised to $1,750.

There are four basic options available when setting up an IRA — a formal trust, a custodial account, an annuity or special Government retirement bonds. In order to provide investment flexibility, an individual can switch his investment from one type of IRA to another without incurring any tax liability. For example, assets put into a trust can be transferred to an annuity (other than an endowment contract), or to Government retirement bonds entirely tax-free.

These rollover rules also apply to lump sum distributions received from any qualified pension or profit-sharing plan. These assets can be put directly into an IRA program without any immediate tax liability. There are several provisions which must be met:

- The lump sum distribution from the qualified plan must be paid to the individual within one year following a) retirement, b) death, c) disability, or d) separation from employment.

- This distribution must then be transferred to the IRA program within 60 days of receipt.

- The amount transferred to the new account cannot include the individual's contributions to the qualified plan. Only company contributions can be rolled over. Since the individual has presumably already paid tax on his contributions, this money can be retained tax-free.

106

- The property transferred to the new IRA account must be the exact same property received from the lump sum distribution. No new assets can be added. If the individual wishes to make additional contributions in the future, a second IRA program must be established, providing the qualifications can be met.

FLOWER BONDS
Discount Bonds Applied At Par Against Estate Taxes

"Flower bonds" are special U.S. Treasury bonds that can be applied at par against estate tax liabilities even though bought at a discount. The number of "flower bonds" available for purchase is shrinking because Congress has prohibited the issue of new bonds carrying this unique provision. Since the ones still outstanding were issued several years ago, the coupon rates are very low by today's standards. Therefore, almost without exception they are selling at substantial discounts from par. The best strategy is to seek those bonds with as deep a discount as possible to take maximum advantage of the tax benefits. However, it is also important to be cognizant of the yields since there is no way of knowing how long you will tie up your assets and, naturally, you want to obtain as much income as possible in the interim.

While "flower bonds" retain much of their appeal, there were some changes resulting from the 1976 tax reform package which have served to reduce the tax advantages. The most important change made the realized difference between par and the higher of the original cost or the price on December 31, 1976 subject to capital gains tax. Under the old rules, the difference between par and the acquisition cost escaped this tax entirely. Secondly, the required holding period to qualify for long term tax treatment is now one year. These provisions apply to all property, but there is no question that they have served to at least partially reduce the advantages of "flower bonds." Still, they can be used to effectively reduce estate tax liabilities.

INDIVIDUAL RETIREMENT ACCOUNT
A Personal Tax Sheltered Pension Program

As a result of the sweeping pension reform bill signed in September of 1974, workers can now establish their own tax-free pension plans. These plans are called Individual Retirement Accounts (IRA). To qualify for an IRA, an individual must be receiving compensation, can be either self-employed or employed by someone else, and cannot be already covered under a tax-sheltered plan. More specifically, an individual is disqualified if he is an active participant in any of the following:

1) a qualified pension, profit-sharing or stock bonus program;

2) a Keogh plan for the self-employed;

3) a qualified annuity plan;

4) a qualified bond purchase plan; or

5) a Government retirement plan.

Once an individual qualifies for an IRA, he can set aside, or an amount can be set aside for him if it is a company program, up to 15% of gross income, to a $1,500 maximum, each year. The tax reform bill of 1976 made a slight liberalization in the contribution limits. The 15% maximum was retained, but the dollar amount was raised to $1,750, providing the IRA is jointly owned by a husband and wife and one of the spouses is not employed. As an alternative, up to $875 can be put in separate accounts, again providing one of the spouses is not employed.

Under the 1978 tax bill, employers have the option of making tax-deductible contributions to an employee's IRA. In this instance, the IRA limits are increased to $7,500 or 15% of earned income. If the employer contributions were less than the normal IRA limits — 15% or $1,500 — the employer could make up the difference to bring the annual amount up to these normal limits.

Under the law, the money set aside in an IRA account is not taxed until distributions are made, presumably at retirement when the individual's tax rate will be lower. Furthermore, the earnings from the account are also tax-free. Depending upon the individual's tax bracket, the benefits of creating such a program can be significant.

Under normal conditions, benefits cannot be withdrawn from an IRA account before age 59-1/2. Distribution must begin not later than the end of the taxable year during which the individual reaches age 70-1/2.

In order to discourage premature withdrawals, stiff penalties have been established. Currently, the penalty is an additional 10% tax on any premature withdrawal. For instance, suppose Mr. White had taxable income of $22,000 for 1976. In addition, he decides to withdraw $1,500 from his Individual Retirement Account. In figuring his tax bill, he would pay the indicated rate on $23,500, plus an additional $150 (10% of the $1,500 withdrawal.)

There are four basic options available to individuals setting up a pension account. The one selected depends entirely on the personal needs of the individual and his family. Regardless of the exact method chosen, however, the contributions are tax-free, as is the income earned on these funds. Below we briefly describe the four basic alternatives available:

- A formal trust can be created, thus giving the money to another party for administration. While the trustee is normally a bank, savings and loan institution or Federally insured credit union, anyone can serve as trustee providing they can demonstrate to the Internal Revenue Service that the money will be held in accordance with the law. The instrument creating the trust must specifically provide that annual contributions will not exceed $1,750; no part of the trust will be invested in insurance contracts; the individual's interest in the trust is nonforfeitable; the assets of the trust will not be commingled except under certain conditions; and distribution of the assets will commence not later than the end of the year in which the individual reaches age 70-1/2.

- An annuity contract can be purchased from a life insurance company. Here, too, there are several stipulations which must be met. The annuity contract cannot be transferable; the annual premium cannot exceed $1,750; the individual's interest cannot be forfeitable; the contract cannot be used as security for a loan; and distributions must begin by age 70-1/2.

- A special custodial account can be created. This is very similar to a trust, although somewhat less formal.

- Finally, special U.S. Government "retirement bonds" can be purchased. These bonds can be bought at any Federal Reserve Bank, any branch or directly from the Treasury. Purchases can be made in denominations of $50, $100 and $500, with an annual yield of 6%, compounded semiannually.

KEOGH PLANS
Tax Sheltered Pension For Self-Employed

The Keogh program was created under the Self-Employed Individuals Tax Retirement Act of 1962. Under the provisions of that act, self-employed individuals were allowed to set aside a percentage of their annual income in a tax-free retirement fund.

Prior to 1974, the maximum yearly contributions to an approved Keogh plan were 10% of earned income, or $2,500, whichever was less. Beginning with taxable years starting after December 31, 1973, the limits were broadened to 15% of earned income, to a maximum of $7,500 each year. While the law sets down rather complicated criteria, generally speaking a self-employed individual is anyone owning more than 10% of a business who qualifies to pay self-employed tax under the Federal social security system.

In order to qualify for a Keogh program, the self-employed employer must establish a retirement plan for all employees. The employer must contribute to the employee program in the same percentage as he contributes to his own plan. For employees to qualify, they must have been employed full-time for at least three years.

Contributions for any year can be made right up to the prescribed date for filing a tax return — April 15 for calendar year taxpayers. It is no longer essential that the payment be made within the fiscal tax year.

One interesting wrinkle of the 1974 changes makes it legal to shelter up to $750 regardless of the percentage limitations. This provision enables a "moonlighter" to set aside income from part-time endeavors, providing the work is conducted on a self-employed basis.

Basically, Keogh funds can be set aside in any of four methods. The one selected depends entirely on individual needs and preferences. Regardless of the particular method selected, however, all contributions are tax deductible and the income earned on the funds accumulates on a tax-free basis. The four approved methods include:

- The creation of a formal trust, thus giving the money to another party to administer. While banks or trust companies are normally selected as trustees, anyone can be chosen as a trustee providing they can demonstrate to the satisfaction of the Internal Revenue Service that the money will be administered in accordance with the law.

- An annuity contract can be purchased from an insurance company (life insurance protection may be included, but only if it is incidental to the retirement benefits).

- A special "custodial account" can be created with a bank, savings and loan or other person. This approach is similar although less formal than a trust.

- Special U.S. Government "retirement bonds" can be purchased.

Normally, benefits may not be withdrawn from Keogh plans before age 59-1/2. Distribution must commence when the covered individual reaches age 70-1/2. The only exceptions to the above rules are in the case of death or permanent disability.

In order to discourage premature withdrawals, penalties are imposed. A 10% penalty is imposed on the amount of the premature withdrawal. Naturally, that is in addition to the normal tax liability.

IT MAY BE TO YOUR ADVANTAGE TO BE EXCLUDED
FROM COMPANY PENSION PLAN

If you do not plan to stay with your present employer, it might be advantageous to seek exclusion from the company sponsored pension plan. One of the vesting options available under the 1974 pension reform law stipulates that an employee must be fully vested after 10 years. Therefore, if you are sure that you will be leaving before full vesting, it might be best to ask your employer to be excluded. Many companies are reluctant to grant such special dispensation out of fear that so many employees will ask to be excluded that the pension plan will lose its qualified status. Still, if approval is granted, you can set up your own Individual Retirement Account (IRA).

MAJOR LIFETIME GIFTS TO CHARITY
Charitable Contributions Can Yield Huge Tax Savings

The minor contributions to charities that we all make from time to time are mostly impulsive acts done just for the joy of giving. But when making gifts of substantial amounts, the tax implications make the gift a significant element in financial planning. Our tax laws encourage charitable giving. When the gift is made to charity, instead of paying a gift tax you are allowed an income tax deduction. Under certain rare circumstances, an individual in a high income tax bracket can actually make more money by giving property away than by selling it. Although your motives may be basically philanthropic, major gifts should be planned to give you the maximum tax savings.

Unfortunately, the Federal gift tax laws are among the most complex of those in the IRS Code. Not only will local taxes vary from state to state, but the Federal rules will also vary depending on the type of charity and property involved. All the reservations and exceptions cannot be covered here, but you should be aware of the general Federal tax rules.

Probably the first thing to check when making a gift is the exact status of the charitable institution according to the IRS. If the charity is not on the approved list, you may wind up increasing rather than decreasing your tax bill. There are three basic categories in which a qualified charity may fall:

Public Charities — These generally include churches, temples, non-profit educational institutions, hospitals and medical research organizations, government units and private operating and distributing foundations. Also included are a broad range of other organiza-

111

tions that have received a substantial amount of public support over a number of years.

Semi-public Charities — These organizations that do not fall in the public charity category include some veteran's, fraternal and non-profit cemetery organizations.

Private Charities — These are private foundations that are not operating or distributing organizations.

Depending on the type of charity and property involved, you are allowed an income tax deduction equal to the value of the gift up to a certain percentage of your adjusted income. Generally, for contributions made to public charities, the deduction per year is limited to 50% of the donor's "contribution base." The contribution base is simply the contributor's adjusted gross income. If the 50% is used up, the remaining amount can be carried over and deducted for the next five years. However, if the 50% is used for contributions to public charities, no deductions are available for contributions to semi-public or private charities.

Contributions to semi-public and private organizations are subject to a 20% limitation, which can be further reduced by any donations to public charities which exceed 30% of an individual's contribution base. There is no carryover permitted for these charities.

There is a special 30% limitation for certain types of property that have appreciated in value while held by the contributor. This 30% applies only if the contribution is made to a public charity. The 20% limitation still applies for the other two categories of charities. However, even with this limitation, contributions of appreciated property often can be made at a lower after-tax cost than other types of property because it may escape the capital gains tax on appreciation.

Every taxpayer who makes a qualified charitable gift is entitled to a tax deduction, but the value of the donation for tax purposes depends on the characteristics of the property involved. Listed securities, for example, are valued at the average between the day's high and low, but are subject to reductions that apply if the sale of the security by the donor would result in a short term gain. For property that has no public auction market, the value is usually defined as the price at which the property would pass between a willing buyer and seller. If the sale of a comparable item has not taken place within a reasonable time of the donation, a recognized appraiser should be consulted. The IRS is not afraid to challenge the claimed value of a gift.

Other special rules may reduce the amount allowable for specific types of property in certain circumstances. If the property is a painting, you may receive a deduction for the full value only if the receiving institution is engaged in a function related to the painting

— such as an art museum. Otherwise, the deduction must be reduced by 50% of the property's appreciation in the hands of the donor.

The contribution is deductible in the year it is paid. Unconditional delivery of the property will be effective as of the date of delivery, while a promissory note is deductible only when it is paid. A contribution of a future interest in property — such as sending a museum a deed that entitles it to receive a painting in a number of years — is not normally deductible until all rights of possession and enjoyment of the property are given up. When these rights are given up, the deduction is based on the current value, not on the value it had when the charity was informed of the gift.

However, a contribution of a future interest in taxpayer's personal residence will provide a contribution deduction to taxpayer in the current year.

USE SHORT TERM LOSSES TO OFFSET ORDINARY INCOME

The Tax Reform Act of 1976 made some important changes in the use of capital losses to offset ordinary income.

First, the required holding period to establish a long term gain or loss has been increased to one year. Secondly, a distinction must now be made between short and long term losses when applied against ordinary income. A $1 short term loss can be applied against ordinary income on a dollar for dollar basis, up to a maximum of $3,000. Therefore, if you have a short term loss of $3,000 during 1978, it can be used to offset $3,000 of income.

Long term losses are treated differently. A $2 long term loss is needed to offset $1 of ordinary income. To obtain the maximum $3,000 offset, long term losses of $6,000 are required.

In effect, short term losses have been given preference over long term losses. Since gains can be offset 100% by either long or short term losses, it is best to use long term losses to offset gains since short term losses can be used dollar for dollar against either capital gains or ordinary income. Unused losses can be carried forward indefinitely.

SHORT SALE AGAINST THE BOX

For those investors possessing large unrealized gains who wish to lock in these profits but postpone the tax liability until the following year, a short sale against the box might be considered. This simple procedure involves selling the particular stock short and then waiting until the following calendar year to complete delivery. While this method cannot be used to convert a short term gain into a long term gain, it is one way to lock in a substantial profit.

It should be noted that this technique assumes that the investor owns the stock. Selling short without owning the security in question is an extremely risky proposition. Additionally, once a short sale against the box has been made, the potential for additional profit should the shares rise in value has been surrendered.

PURCHASING VALUABLE ASSETS WITH BORROWED MONEY

Despite today's high interest rates, it still may make good sense to use borrowed money to purchase assets which are likely to appreciate in value — real estate, securities, works of art, diamonds, etc. Subject to the limitations delineated below, the interest paid on such loans is fully deductible (unless used to buy tax-free municipals or certain other investment assets). No tax liability is incurred on the appreciating value of the property in question, either. Should such property eventually be sold, the gain will be taxed at more favorable capital gains rates.

There are limitations on the deduction of investment interest. The deduction by noncorporate taxpayers is limited to $10,000 per year, plus the taxpayer's net investment income. The $10,000 figure is reduced to $5,000 for a married person filing a separate return and to zero in the case of a trust. Interest deductions over the maximum are entitled to an unlimited carryover and may be deducted in future years subject to the annual limits.

For a borrower in the 50% tax bracket, the interest deduction would effectively cut his borrowing costs in half. Money borrowed at 10% would really cost the taxpayer only 5%.

THE INSTALLMENT SALE
Spread Out Capital Gains Liability

An installment sale allows the holder of a highly appreciated asset (most often common stocks or real estate) to spread a large capital gains tax liability over a number of years. Unfortunately, all too many investors are inclined to hold a highly appreciated asset solely because of the unattractive tax consequences of liquidation. The installment sale can provide a solution to this dilemma.

The requirements of a proper installment sale are:

1) Payments received in the year the property is sold must not exceed 30% of the total selling price.

2) The purchaser must make at least two payments which fall in two separate tax years.

3) The selling price must exceed $1,000.

4) The sale must be properly indicated on the seller's tax return for the year in which the sale is executed.

5) Simple interest of not less than 6% should be applied to the installment note.

To illustrate the tax advantages, a simple example can be used. Suppose Mr. A owns a piece of real estate with a cost basis of $10,000 and a current market value of $100,000. To sell outright would result in a substantial tax bite. Instead, he could sell the property to Mr. B, payable $10,000 down and in nine additional annual payments of $10,000, plus 6% interest on the unpaid balance. Of the $10,000 annual installments, $1,000 is nontaxable as a return of capital and $9,000 is subject to a capital gains tax. Naturally, the interest is taxable as ordinary income.

In the above example, Mr. B can dispose of the property in any manner he sees fit, providing there was not a prearranged plan to resell the property to a third party for full payment in the year of the sale. The IRS has consistently held that a sale by one person cannot be transformed for tax purposes into a sale by another by using the latter as a conduit to pass title to a third party through a prearranged agreement.

CHARITABLE REMAINDER TRUST
Combine Charitable Contribution With Tax Savings

Many people, either during their lifetime or in their will, provide bequests to their favorite charities. But in doing so, many of these same people ignore the advantages of a charitable remainder trust. These trusts offer a way to donate assets to charity and receive a tax deduction while still receiving income from the assets.

A charitable remainder trust is an arrangement made with a charity in which you donate money or property in trust to the charity in return for an income to you or to your wife for as long as you live. Then at your death, the gift becomes the sole property of the charity. More than one charity can be involved, and the income can be paid to someone other than yourself.

Here's one example of how it can work: Mr. Smith, the donor, establishes a charitable remainder trust with his school in which he places common stocks that were purchased many years ago at prices substantially below current market value. The income from these stocks is paid to Mr. Smith as beneficiary, and at his death the income payments stop and his school receives the property.

Mr. Smith will thus receive an immediate income tax deduction for the gift, escape the capital gains tax, reduce his estate taxes by effectively removing the gift property from his estate, receive income payments during his lifetime, and still benefit his alma mater.

There are three varieties of charitable remainder trusts:

Annuity — In this arrangement, a fixed dollar amount is paid to the beneficiary on a monthly, quarterly, semiannual or yearly basis. The beneficiary must be living when the trust is created, and the yearly payments must amount to at least 5% of the market value of the gift property at the time it was donated. Payments can last a specified term of 20 years or less, or can last for the life of the beneficiary.

Unitrust — Instead of a fixed amount, a fixed percentage is paid. This percentage is applied to the market value of the trust's assets at the beginning of each year. Thus, the actual amount paid will depend on the fluctuating value of the gift each year. The percentage must again be 5% or more, and the duration limits are the same as for the annuity type.

Pooled Income Fund — In this type the charity pools your donation with other similar donations and administers the fund itself. The charity pays a share of the income generated to each donor, operating much like a mutual fund. The amount of the payments will again vary year to year. At your death, the charity removes your share from the fund to use for its own purposes.

The amount you are allowed as a charitable deduction depends, among other things, on the type of the trust. The pooled income fund allows the largest portion of the gift to be deductible. Federal tables are used to calculate the deduction based on the age of the donor and the percentage of the income payments. All other things equal, the older the person is and the lower the income payments, the larger the deduction. However, this is limited to 30% of the adjusted gross income of the donor when the gift is an appreciated asset, and 50% when the property is nonappreciated (such as cash). If necessary, the deductible amount can be carried over for five years.

The charitable deduction is, of course, determined in the year the trust is created, and is based on the estimated present value of the charity's future interest in the gift. Even if the charity receives an amount greater or less than calculated, no additional adjustments will be made.

The trust itself is tax-exempt. Only the beneficiary who receives the income payments is taxed, with the payments regarded as ordinary income. However, if the beneficiary is in a high tax bracket, his income payments can be received free of tax if a unitrust is established that invests only in tax-exempt bonds.

In all cases, a qualified charity must receive the remainder of the gift after payments to the beneficiary are completed. The Internal Revenue Service has specific requirements for a qualified charity. Except for the pooled income fund trust, the charity need not be aware of the existence of the trust, and a charity can be added or dropped during the life of the trust. This is the only thing, however, that can be changed once the trust is established. You give up all legal rights to the property itself in the trust.

If the trust property is exhausted before the expiration date of the trust, there is no further obligation due the beneficiary, so an individual's needs should be considered in determining the terms of the trust.

PRIVATE ANNUITIES
A Transfer Of Property Among Family Members

A rarely used estate planning tool that recently has been gaining in popularity is the family or private annuity. The basic idea, as with all annuities, is to transfer property from one person (the annuitant) to another (the obligor) in exchange for a promise to pay the annuitant a specific income for the rest of his life or a specific number of years. The private annuity differs from a commercial annuity in that the private annuity most often occurs between family members and the arrangement is not secured in any way.

A private annuity is usually used between a child and one or both parents. For example, Mr. Smith, who is near retirement, and Mrs. Smith want their son, who is in a lower tax bracket, to inherit their entire estate at their death. The Smiths also want to change their jointly owned stock portfolio from growth stocks to more income oriented issues. Under a private annuity arrangement, the stocks are transferred to the son, who then makes the switch to income stocks. The son then promises to make regular monthly payments to his parents that will amount to the present value of the property, which is calculated from Federal annuity tables. When the parents die, the payments stop and the son has no further obligation to the estate.

The major advantage of this arrangement is that estate taxes will be reduced because the stock assets are removed from the estate. This is the most common reason for using private annuities. But Mr. Smith will also benefit because no immediate capital gains tax will be incurred. The liability will instead be spread over a number of years. In addition, the gift tax will be avoided and the family's income tax probably will be reduced.

The income tax treatment of the payments received by the annuitant depends on the circumstances of each case. However, in most cases part of the payment is a return of capital and therefore

117

tax-free, part is taxable as a capital gain and part is treated as ordinary income. Usually, this treatment will result in less of a tax liability than if the annuity arrangement was not used.

For the obligor, any income derived from the transferred property is taxable to him, and he is not entitled to a deduction for any portion of the payments he makes to the annuitant. Obviously, income tax advantages to the family as a whole can only result if the obligor is in a lower tax bracket than the annuitant. The obligor also faces some contingent tax liabilities on any capital gains that may occur during the period after the property transfer since the property will, in fact, belong to him.

In some cases gift taxes may also be incurred. The original annuity transfer in the Smith's example could have been subject to gift taxes if the property had not been jointly owned. Mrs. Smith's interest in the annuity then would have been considered a gift to her made by Mr. Smith.

Gift taxes may also be levied if the annual annuity payment is a different figure than that computed on the basis of Government life expectancy tables. For example, if the tables indicate that a 70 year old man who transfers $80,000 of property to the obligor should receive a $10,000 annual annuity payment, any variation will result in a gift tax liability. If he receives $12,000 per year, the extra $2,000 is a taxable gift for which the obligor is responsible. If the payments are less than the table indicates, the annuitant might then be liable for gift taxes.

The greatest tax advantage of the private annuity is the avoidance of estate taxes. Since the annuity arrangement ends at the death of the annuitant, it has no value when the death occurs and should not be included in his estate. If the value of the transferred property equals that of the annuity so that there are no gift taxes, there will also be no estate taxes. The only exception might occur if there are joint beneficiaries. In this case, if the first beneficiary should die before his income payments amount to the estimated actuarial value of the annuity, then the excess will be included in the decedent's estate.

There are several factors that must be watched when making the annuity transaction in order to insure that the IRS does not attack the annuity as a sham. A written health report on the annuitant should be obtained to prove the transaction was not made in contemplation of death or based on inaccurate actuarial computations. In many cases it is also advisable to have the property appraised.

Insurance should be considered for both the annuitant and the obligor. The obligor may want insurance on the annuitant to offset possible tax liabilities should the annuitant die prematurely, and the annuitant may want insurance on the obligor to insure that payments continue if he (the obligor) should die first. However, the insurance should not be mentioned in the actual annuity agreement because negative tax implications might result. It might be wise, though, to prohibit the obligor by contract from issuing another annuity while yours continues.

One of the most significant problems with the annuity is the question of the ability of the obligor to maintain the computed annuity payments. Because the annuity payments theoretically contain a partial return of capital, the required income payments frequently are more than the net income derived from the property. Therefore, the obligor must be able to afford making up the difference.

One way to solve this problem, assuming the annuitant has sufficient wealth, would be for the annuitant to transfer some property for an annuity and some additional property as an outright gift. Made in the proper amounts, the gift tax credit would eliminate tax liabilities on the gift and the annuity would remain a tax-free transfer. The income from the gift plus the annuity property should be sufficient to cover the annuity payments.

MILEAGE ALLOWANCE
Deduct Unreimbursed Costs Or $0.18½ A Mile

Anyone who uses his car for business purposes is allowed a legitimate deduction for unreimbursed expenses. Currently, there are two basic options available. The first would be to claim all unreimbursed operating expenses of the car. This includes gas, oil, repairs, license plates, insurance and depreciation.

The second opinion is to take a flat mileage allowance of $0.18½ a mile for the first 15,000 miles and $0.10 for mileage above 15,000. The person who opts for the flat allowance can also take a deduction for interest and taxes associated with the purchase of the car. Previously, the IRS allowed no credit for interest and taxes unless deductions were itemized. Those taking the standard deduction lost out. This position has been modified.

SINGLE-PREMIUM DEFERRED ANNUITIES
Defer Tax Liability On Retirement Fund

If you are searching for ways to provide for a retirement that is still a few years off, you may want to consider an annuity. Basically, annuities are arrangements made with an insurance company in which the policyholder is guaranteed annual or more frequent payments for the duration of his life. These payments consist of a return of the original capital plus interest.

One version of an annuity, called a single-premium deferred annuity, is especially suited for retirement plans. Here's an example of how it works: Mr. Smith, for a single payment of $10,000, purchases a deferred annuity when he is 55 years old. When Mr. Smith reaches age 65, he will begin to receive a guaranteed monthly payment for the rest of his life. The basic advantage is that all interest earned during the 10 years prior to retirement is allowed to accumulate tax-free. The savings can be significant, depending on your tax bracket.

Mr. Smith's payment at age 55 and accumulated interest will provide the fund that will subsequently be used to purchase the actual annuity. During this period before retirement, the interest that accumulates will not be taxable provided any withdrawals from the fund are not in excess of the original investment. Although these limited withdrawals can be made tax-free, insurance companies will frequently charge a percentage penalty if a withdrawal is made in the early years. This penalty is used to discourage investors from using the policies as temporary investments.

Some policies will allow cancellation in advance of the starting date of income payments without penalty if the company's current interest rate falls below a specified level. The interest then becomes taxable the year the policy is cancelled.

After this accumulation period is over and the fund is converted into an annuity paying a steady income, the part of the income payment that resulted from interest earnings becomes subject to tax. Provided the annuity was not created through a pension plan, the part which consists of a return of your capital remains tax-free. Tables are provided by the Internal Revenue Service to compute what percentage of the income payments is interest and therefore taxable.

Insurance companies pay interest on the policy during the accumulation period. The rate fluctuates with the rate of return on investments made with the money. If the investments yield more, the policyholder receives more. If yields decline, a minimum rate is still guaranteed, although the guarantee is usually only about 3% or 4%.

While some companies sell the policies without any sales or administration fees, others will charge a percentage of the premium or a flat amount. Lately, many insurance firms have been selling single-premium deferred annuity contracts through brokerage houses as well as insurance agents.

When the initial accumulation period is over at retirement, your policy gives you the right to use its cash value to purchase the actual annuity plan that makes income payments. The amount of these payments is at the rate stated in the policy contract or at the rate in effect when you actually convert. It is possible, although rarely done, to transfer the policy to purchase an annuity plan from another company without tax complications.

The plans usually available to you are:

Straight — In this plan you receive the stipulated income payments for as long as you live, and the payments stop at your death.

Cash Refund — This plan also gives you life payments, but if you die before the payments add up to the original purchase price, the remainder will be paid to your named beneficiary.

Guaranteed Number of Payments — Similar to the cash refund plan, here a certain number of years of payments are guaranteed. If you should die before the stipulated number of years, your beneficiary will receive the payments for the remainder of the period. Plans for 5, 10, 15 or 20 years are available.

Joint and Survivor — Two people, usually a husband and wife, receive payments that continue after the death of the first. Depending on the plan, the survivor will receive the same or reduced payments. This plan might also be combined with a guaranteed number of payments.

Besides the type of plan you select, other factors will affect the cost. Women, because of their longer life spans, must pay more than men. If the annuity is purchased through a pension plan approved by the IRS, the cost will be less because the insurance company receives favorable tax treatment. There are also differences in rates among companies making it worthwhile to compare before you purchase.

One big weakness of the deferred annuity is that it, like all fixed investments, does not offset losses in purchasing power due to inflation. Still, an income of depreciated dollars is better than no income at all, so for the person who wishes to be protected against his own inability to handle money, the deferred annuity has its advantages. And, of course, those who live beyond the life expectancy assigned to them will get a higher than anticipated return.

One option open to those individuals who are not satisfied to receive a fixed monthly amount is the variable annuity. The variable annuity guarantees an income for life, but the amount of the monthly payments is not rigid because it is based largely on equity (stock) investments. In the case of a conventional annuity, the fund is invested exclusively in fixed income instruments. While the variable annuity allows for the potential of keeping up with inflation, it also exposes the holder to substantially increased risk.

Those who want a steady, secure monthly amount should stick with a conventional annuity.

TRAVEL AND ENTERTAINMENT DEDUCTIONS
Accurate, Thorough Records Essential

Recently, travel and entertainment deductions have become a very controversial issue. The Internal Revenue Service is taking a much closer look at this often abused area.

Basically, such expenses are deductible if they are reasonable and necessary expenses directly connected with, and necessary or appropriate to, the pursuit of a trade, business or profession. Expenses that are lavish or extravagant under the circumstances are not deductible.

To insure that legitimate expenses are not thrown out, it is imperative that good records be kept. There are four principal pieces of information that are essential:

- The amount of the expenditure.
- The time and place of the expenditure.
- The business purpose of the expense.
- The business relationship of the parties involved.

Deductions for traveling are acceptable if they are associated with attending a convention directly related to the taxpayer's trade or business. It is also an allowable deduction if the traveling expenses are in connection with looking after or inspecting business or investment interests.

When a trip is taken which combines personal and business activities, the likelihood of close IRS scrutiny is even greater. If the trip was taken primarily for business reasons, the traveling expenses must be allocated between the time spent for business and the time spent for personal purposes. Only the expenses directly related to the business purpose are deductible. If the trip was taken primarily for personal reasons, the traveling expenses are not deductible.

AN AMENDED RETURN
Don't Hesitate To Correct An Inaccurate Return

Many individuals file their Federal tax return, only to learn later that they failed to take advantage of an allowable deduction. It is a very simple procedure to file an amended return by using Form 1040X. The taxpayer simply indicates the change and recomputes the amount of tax payable or refund due. While it is a relatively simple procedure, many seem reluctant to do so. There is an ingrained fear that such action may prompt the IRS to more closely scrutinize the original return. Since there is no evidence that this is the case, it is foolish not to make the small effort to file an amended return if an error has been made.

AN IRREVOCABLE TRUST
Tax Benefits Through Permanent Transfer Of Property

The irrevocable trust has many advantages that make it an attractive financial planning tool. It can reduce family income and estate taxes, avoid probate and assure professional management of property. However, these advantages are available only if you are willing to, in effect, give property away to someone else.

Basically, a trust is a legal arrangement in which one person, the grantor, transfers property to someone else, the trustee, who then administers the property for the benefit of a third party, the beneficiary. What makes the trust irrevocable is the fact that the grantor cannot terminate the trust once it is established, and must therefore generally give up all legal rights to the property.

Perhaps the best situation in which to use an irrevocable trust is in the following example. A father has a substantial estate that he wishes his son to receive at his death. However, he is concerned with his son's inability to handle his own personal finances, and fears his son will spend a gift or inheritance foolishly. So, the father puts a substantial amount of common stock into an irrevocable trust with his son as beneficiary. In the trust document he stipulates that any income generated by the stock be immediately distributed to his son, while the stock itself be liquidated at the discretion of the trustee only under specific circumstances.

Besides assuring that the property is professionally managed by naming a competent trustee, the trust, if properly set up, transfers the tax liability on the income generated by the trust principal (corpus) to the son, who is probably in a lower tax bracket. However, because the father has given up control of the property, a gift subject to tax has occurred. The only control the father has is in the imposition of conditions on the use of the gift. These conditions must be carefully limited to insure that the property is not included in his estate. To escape estate taxes, the IRS requires that the grantor relinquish all power over the property, no matter how slight.

Because the property is removed from the father's estate, not only are estate taxes reduced, but so are costs that would be incurred in probating the property. There are several reasons for wanting to avoid probate. First, secrecy can be maintained. When a will is probated, certain details are made public as the will becomes a matter of public record. The size of the estate, the names of beneficiaries, as well as what they get and on what terms, will be revealed. An irrevocable trust can keep these details secret. Second, appraisers and guardians may also be required in probate. Third, probate results in a certain amount of delay, which a trust avoids. Finally, the more property in the estate, the higher the fees of the executor and legal counsel.

Setting up a trust involves legal and trustee fees, but for large estates they are not likely to be as high as those involved in probate. These costs must be compared, along with possible savings in income and estate taxes. As a general rule, estates must be worth over $150,000 to make such a trust worthwhile.

Generally, if you set up an irrevocable trust you will not, as grantor, be taxed on any income it generates if it meets the following conditions:

1) You do not receive any income the property generates.

2) It does not support someone you are legally obligated to support.

3) It is not used to meet any of your legal obligations.

4) The income is not accumulated for you.

5) It is not used to pay premiums on an insurance policy on your life.

If the trust does meet these requirements, it can usually be used to divert income to someone in a lower tax bracket, such as a son, and provide overall family tax savings.

GIFT GIVING TO FAMILY MEMBERS
Advantages For Both Giver And Recipient

Many people fail to take full advantage of the opportunities available from gift giving. While considerable forethought should be given before making a final decision, once it is determined that you can afford to make a gift, it is often advantageous to do so.

First, by giving away income producing property you will serve to reduce your own income tax liability. Secondly, once the asset has been given away, it is effectively removed from your estate. Therefore, gift giving results in both short term and long term tax benefits.

Despite major changes in the treatment of gift giving as a result of the 1976 Tax Reform Act, the $3,000 annual exclusion was left unchanged. This means that you can give $3,000 a year to as many people as you wish without any tax liability. If you are married, you

and your wife can make a combined gift of $6,000 per year per recipient.

In addition to the annual exclusion, there is a lifetime unified tax credit. The credit rises from $34,000 in 1978 to $47,000 in 1981 and beyond. In essence the unified credit can be used to offset either gift or estate taxes. It must be remembered, however, that if you use part or all of your unified credit to make gifts above the annual exclusion, it will reduce the credit available when you die.

MARITAL GIFT EXEMPTION
Special Exemption For Gifts To Spouse

In addition to the normal gift giving provisions outlined above, $100,000 can be given to a spouse without gift tax liability. This is a lifetime amount and it need not be used up at the same time. After the first $100,000 is used up, the next $100,000 in gifts to a spouse will be fully taxable. Once $200,000 in gifts has been made to a spouse, only half of anything given thereafter will be subject to gift tax. Obviously, however, any gifting to a spouse should be done only after careful consideration has been given to other estate planning ramifications.

THE MARITAL DEDUCTION

Once an estate comes within its domain, the Federal estate tax is likely to be the largest source of expense related to the transfer of property at death. For a married couple, the easiest and most effective way to reduce this expense is through the use of the marital deduction. Basically, the marital deduction allows you to leave the greater of (a) $250,000 or (b) one half of your estate (after deducting debts, funeral expenses and costs of administration) to your spouse free from estate tax. However, this is just the general rule, and there are exceptions and qualifications that open up both opportunities and pitfalls.

Before using this approach, it must be determined whether it is wise to fully use the marital deduction. Although it is available, you are not required to use the maximum allowed. Tax and nontax considerations could make it advisable to use only part of the deduction.

If the only consideration is to receive the maximum estate tax savings in the estate of the first spouse to die, then the full use of the marital deduction would be wise in most cases. But you might also want to look at the resulting situation for the survivor and her estate tax liability.

Suppose the husband had a gross estate of $350,000 and his wife had no estate of her own. If the husband had made full use of the marital deduction in his will, $250,000 in this case, and left the rest in a nonmarital trust, he would escape any Federal estate tax. But his wife's estate, assuming she kept the $250,000 intact, would be hit with a substantial tax on that amount when she dies. If the husband instead had made a qualified marital deduction of $175,000, and put the rest in a marital trust to pay income to his wife and the remainder to the children, neither his nor her estate would have to pay any Federal estate tax. This is because of the availability of a unified credit. The unified credit replaces the $30,000 lifetime gift exemption and the $60,000 estate tax exemption. Any part of the credit used to offset gift taxes will not be available to offset estate tax liabilities.

UNIFIED CREDIT		
Year	Credit	Equivalent Exemption
1978	$34,000	$134,000
1979	38,000	147,333
1980	42,500	161,563
1981 and after	47,000	175,625

When it is fully phased in by 1981, the unified credit will provide a $47,000 credit which can be used against both estate and gift taxes which would otherwise have to be paid. The new law also provides for an unlimited gift tax deduction for the first $100,000 of lifetime gifts made to one's spouse, with a 50% deduction for gifts in excess of $200,000. However, the use of the 50% deduction on gifts reduces the amount of the marital deduction that will be allowed on estate taxes.

A potential problem with the marital deduction may arise when a husband and wife execute joint and mutual wills under terms which obligate the survivor to make bequests to certain persons. If state law prohibits the survivor from revoking the will or making a different disposition, the bequest received by the survivor will not qualify for the marital deduction.

The situation in which both spouses die within a short time of one another or at the same time also deserves special consideration. In both of these situations the property may needlessly be subject to taxation under both estates. This problem may be avoided by a condition being placed on the bequest that requires the spouse to survive the deceased by six months or more in order to receive the gift. If the spouse does actually survive that period, the marital deduction will be allowable.

MUNICIPAL BONDS
One Of The Safest Of All Tax Shelters

While tax-free bonds don't offer the opportunity for huge tax write-offs like some of the esoteric tax shelters, they do provide the high tax bracket individual with a sure-fire way to substantially improve his return on a basically secure investment.

Specifically, municipal bonds are those debt instruments issued by public agencies below the level of the Federal Government — including states, counties, cities, school districts, housing authorities, etc. These issues are free from Federal, and in some cases, state and local taxes.

While municipal bonds normally provide a lower coupon yield than do fully taxable bonds, the tax-exempt status proves more than compensatory for those individuals in elevated tax brackets. For someone in a 50% tax bracket, a 5% coupon would be equivalent to a taxable coupon of 10%.

UNIT TRUSTS
Capital Returned On Self-Liquidating Basis

Municipal unit trusts, which have been in existence since 1961, are in many respects similar to the more recent municipal bond funds. There are some important distinctions, however. While they also pool investor capital to purchase a diversified portfolio of municipal bonds, there is no attempt made at managing the portfolio once assembled. As the various bonds mature, the principal is returned to the trust participants on a self-liquidating basis. Unit trusts are sold normally in $1,000 units rather than in share form.

These self-liquidating funds, most of which are sponsored by major brokerage firms, assess an initial sales charge usually averaging between 3-1/2% and 4-1/2%. The portfolio is administered by a trustee, normally a bank. While the issuer generally maintains a secondary market for their units, there is no legal obligation to do so. As a backup, the trustee will normally redeem the units at net asset value.

MUNICIPAL BOND FUNDS
Diversification, But Not Without A Price

As outlined above, municipal bonds do represent one of the safest of all tax shelters. Buying individual bonds does have some drawbacks, however. First, municipals often lack liquidity. If the holder finds it necessary to sell before maturity, he might be forced to make a substantial price concession. Furthermore, it may be very difficult for the small investor to achieve sufficient diversification. Like any investment, it is best to spread your risks around with municipal bonds. Finally, there is the question of choice. Many potential investors have great difficulty in properly assessing the relative appeal of the thousands of municipal issues outstanding.

Because of these potential drawbacks, municipal bond funds have become extremely popular the past few years. Prior to 1976, mutual funds could not pass on tax-free income to their investors even though the income was tax-free for the fund. As a result of the Tax Reform Act of 1976, this was all changed.

The municipal bond funds operate essentially the same as a common stock mutual fund. Most are no-load, although a few do assess an initial sales charge. All investments are pooled together to purchase municipal bonds. The bond portfolio is managed, with changes made on a regular basis. The concept provides maximum liquidity since investments can be redeemed whenever desired based on the current net asset value of the portfolio. Since the municipal bond funds are managed, a regular management fee is assessed against the portfolio.

SAVINGS BONDS DEFER TAX LIABILITIES
Series EE Bonds Allow Interest To Accumulate Tax-Free

While many people don't recognize it, U.S. Savings bonds offer unique tax advantages. Presently, savings bonds are issued in two series, EE and HH. Series EE bonds are sold in denominations of $50, $75, $100, $200, $500, $1,000, $5,000 and $10,000. They are purchased at a 50% discount from face value — a $100 bond would cost $50. Interest accrues at a rate of 6½%, compounded semi-annually, if the bond is held at least five years. If cashed earlier than five years after issue, the yield will be less.

EE bonds can be converted (at redemption value) to HH bonds anytime after they have been held for six months.

Interest on HH bonds is paid semi-annually by treasury check at a level rate of 6½%. If the HH bonds are cashed in before being held five years, the current redemption value will be less than the face amount.

Savings bonds, both EE and HH are exempt from state and local taxes like all government obligations. Because the EE bonds mature in 11 years, it is no longer possible to defer interest for decades as was possible under the former E bonds which are no longer being sold.

DEPRECIATION
A Tax Break Available To Individuals As Well As Corporations

While most people think that depreciation deductions are limited to huge corporations, there are many applications where the individual can enjoy significant tax benefits. For example, if you own rental property, it may be depreciated. Many professionals (accountants, lawyers, physicians) can recover the cost of books and certain other equipment through depreciation deductions.

Depreciation is defined as wear and tear on property used in a trade or business. In order to take a depreciation deduction for income tax purposes, only certain kinds of property qualify. For instance, you cannot claim depreciation on land, stock, bonds or securities. Depreciation is not allowable for property used for personal purposes, such as a residence or an automobile used solely for pleasure. Depreciation is allowable for tangible property, but not for an inventory, stock in trade or depletable natural resource. An intangible asset such as a patent, copyright, franchise or license is depreciable, but good will is not.

Although the Internal Revenue Service does not prescribe any specific method of depreciation, it must be a reasonable plan and the burden of proof rests with the taxpayer. Therefore, full and complete records are essential.

Additionally, a taxpayer must deduct the proper depreciation allowance in each year. If he fails to deduct depreciation or deducts an amount which is inadequate under the facts known at the time, he cannot take advantage of it in later years.

As noted previously, there are no set methods of depreciation required. The most often used technique is called straight-line depreciation. Very simply, straight-line depreciation assumes that the asset wears out uniformly during its useful life. For example, if you had a $100 piece of machinery with an estimated life of 10 years and no scrap value, 10%, or $10 per year, could be deducted as depreciation.

Another technique for depreciating property is the so-called sum of digits method. This method, which was authorized by Congress beginning in 1954, allows for an acceleration in depreciation. A simple example will illustrate how this method works. Suppose a piece of equipment costs $1,000, has a useful life of five years and no scrap value. The sum of digits is $1 + 2 + 3 + 4 + 5 = 15$. In the first year, 5/15 of the $1,000 cost could be deducted. In the next year, 4/15 would be deducted. In the fifth year, 1/15 deduction would remain. Under no circumstances can a piece of property be depreciated below its salvage or scrap value.

These are just two of the various techniques of depreciating property. Clearly, this is a rather complicated field which requires professional guidance. When properly utilized, however, depreciation can be a major source of tax savings.

THE DIVIDEND EXCLUSION
Up To $200 Annual Exclusion On Joint Returns

The first $100 of dividend income received by an individual, estate or trust from a taxable domestic corporation is excluded from gross income. With this single exception, taxpayers must include in their gross income the full amount of dividends received from either a domestic corporation or a foreign corporation. On jointly-owned stocks, the dividends are considered as received one-half by each owner. Therefore, on a joint return, each spouse may exclude the first $100 of eligible dividends. If one spouse has dividend income of more than $100 while the other has none, the exclusion is still $100. If each spouse has dividend income of $100 or more, the maximum exclusion is then doubled to $200.

The annual dividend exclusion does not apply in the following cases:

- a China Trade Act corporation;
- an exempt corporation, including a farmers' cooperative in the exempt classification;
- a corporation deriving most of its income from U.S. possessions;
- a tax-option corporation;
- a real estate investment trust.

INVESTORS' EXPENSES PARTIALLY DEDUCTIBLE
Many Taxpayers Fail To Deduct Investment Related Expenses

An individual, estate or trust may deduct reasonable, ordinary and necessary expenses closely related to, and paid or incurred in, the following activities:

- The production or collection of income.
- Management, conservation or maintenance of property held for income production.
- Determination, collection or refund of any tax.

These expenses may be deducted even though not connected with a trade, business or profession.

Various types of legal and other professional advice fall in the deductible category. The test is that this advice has something to do with the production, adjustment, management or maintenance of an income producing investment. This is one area where there tend to be various interpretational shadings. Clearly, not all legal or professional fees are allowable deductions.

Some other deductible expenses are investment advisory and management fees; transfer taxes; expenses incurred in looking after income-producing property; insurance and storage charges for merchandise bought and held as a speculative investment; safe deposit box rental (providing it is not used for personal effects or tax-exempt securities).

DEPLETION
A Special Allowance For Wasting Assets

In simplest terms, depletion is to natural resources what depreciation is to equipment or real estate. Minerals, petroleum, timber and other natural deposits are wasting assets. The gradual reduction of the original source by removal is known as depletion. The law allows for a deduction to compensate the owner of such depleting assets.

Only an individual or a corporation that is the sole owner and operator of the property can deduct depletion for that property. A deduction may be allowed, however, to more than one taxpayer if the owner is a trust or partnership, or has transferred part of his economic interest in the resource to another.

The basic method of computing depletion is "cost depletion." The basis upon which the deduction is allowed is the adjusted basis of the property. Determination of cost depletion requires first an estimate of the number of units (tons, barrels, etc.) which make up the deposit. Then that part of the cost or other adjusted basis of the property which is allocable to the depletable reserves is divided by the number of units. The quotient is the cost depletion per unit. This amount, multiplied by the number of units extracted or sold during the year, determines the cost depletion deductible for the year. Each year the cost basis of the property is reduced, but not below zero, by the amount of depletion deducted for that year. The remaining basis is used in computing cost depletion for the next year.

Much like depreciation, depletion is a rather complicated concept. The Internal Revenue Service has set down precise guidelines for its application. It would be virtually impossible for an individual to sit down and accurately compute annual depletion deductions without professional assistance.

EDUCATIONAL EXPENSES

Some, but by no means all, education related expenses are deductible. To qualify, the education must be undertaken:

- to maintain or improve a skill required by the individual in his employment;

- to meet the expressed requirements of the individual's employer, or;

- to satisfy the requirements of law or regulations, imposed as a condition to the retention by the individual of an established employment relationship, status or rate of compensation.

Educational expenses which are personal in nature are not deductible even though they may indirectly maintain or improve a skill or meet the expressed requirement of the taxpayer's employer. Nondeductible education expenses are those which: (1) are required in order to meet the minimum educational requirements for qualification by the taxpayer in his present employment, trade or business; or (2) qualify the taxpayer for a new trade or business.

The 1978 tax bill made all employer provided education help tax-free for five years, starting January 1, 1979. This break does not apply to living expenses or courses involving sports, games or hobbies.

MOVING EXPENSES
Expenses Related To Move To New Job Location Deductible

An employee or self-employed person who moves to a new job location can deduct both the direct and indirect costs of moving. Direct costs include:

- The cost of transporting the taxpayer and members of his household from the old to the new residence.

- The cost of transporting their household goods and personal effects.

- The cost of meals and lodging in route.

These direct moving expenses are fully deductible, assuming they are reasonable and not excessive.

Indirect moving costs include:

- Temporary living expenses (up to 30 days) at a new job location.

- Expenses of traveling between the old principal residence and new place of employment for the purpose of searching for a new residence.

- Expenses incident to a sale, purchase or lease of a residence.

These indirect deductions are limited to a total amount of $3,000, with expenses related to house hunting trips and temporary living expenses at the new job location not to exceed $1,500.

To qualify as a legitimate deduction, two tests must be met. First, the new job must be at least 35 miles further from the old home than the old job was from the old home. Secondly, the employee must be a full-time employee in the general location of his new place of employment for at least 39 weeks of the 12 month period immediately following his arrival in that general location.

Any amount received, directly or indirectly, by a taxpayer from his employer as a payment or reimbursement of expenses of moving from one residence to another must be included in the taxpayer's gross income as compensation for services. The employee is then permitted to deduct his expenses to the extent to which they qualify as deductible moving expenses.

INCOME AVERAGING
A Way To Compensate For Unusual Income Swings

Any taxpayer who experiences unusual fluctuations in income can use an averaging formula to ease the tax burden in peak income years. Income averaging rules apply to almost all types of income, including salaries, commissions, bonuses, interest, dividends, professional fees, capital gains, wagering income, income from gifts or inheritance and income from sole proprietorships or partnerships. The only two sources of income that do not qualify for averaging are premature payouts from self-employed retirement plans and accumulation distributions from trusts.

To qualify for income averaging, the "averagable income" must be more than $3,000. The formula for averaging is rather complicated. First, the excess of the income for the current taxable year over 120% of the average annual income over the four preceding years is calculated. This excess is the amount subject to averaging (averagable income). If this amount does not equal at least $3,000, you do not qualify for averaging. The tax is computed for one-fifth of the averagable income and multiplied by five to find the tax on this income. The tax on the non-averagable income is added to this amount, and the total is the tax liability for the year.

EMPLOYEE DEATH BENEFITS
Up To $5,000 Exempt From Tax

Up to $5,000 of any death benefit paid by or for an employer can be excluded from the gross income of the beneficiaries. The aggregate exclusion for any one employee is $5,000. If benefits totaling more than $5,000 are received by more than one beneficiary, the excludable portion will be allocated among them.

If the death benefits are paid in installments, the first $5,000 of installments is excluded. The remainder is fully taxable. The total exclusion cannot exceed $5,000 even if payments are made by more than one employer.

There is no exclusion for amounts to which the employee had a vested right. Neither is there an exclusion for death payments resulting from a self-employed retirement plan.

CASUALTY LOSSES
Subject to $100 Limitation

Casualty losses resulting from fire, flood, storm, shipwreck, theft or vandalism are fully deductible, subject to some limitations. By definition, a casualty is the complete or partial destruction or loss of property resulting from an identifiable event that is damaging to the property, and sudden, unexpected or unusual in nature.

For the purposes of this discussion, we will limit our remarks to personal casualty losses. The amount of the casualty loss deduction is generally the lesser of:

- the decrease in the fair market value of the property as a result of the casualty; or

- your adjusted basis in the property.

This amount must then be reduced by any insurance or other recovery. Furthermore, all personal casualty losses are subject to a $100 limitation. Specifically, that means that the first $100 of loss is not deductible.

A casualty deduction is allowed for damage (in excess of $100) to a pleasure automobile resulting from a collision, whether due to the faulty driving of another or the taxpayer, if damage caused by the taxpayer is not due to his willful act.

ALIMONY VERSUS CHILD SUPPORT
The Tax Consequences Are Quite Different

Alimony, separate maintenance or similar periodic payments that one makes to a spouse or former spouse are an allowable tax deduction for the one making the payments. For the recipient, such payments are viewed as taxable income.

Child support payments, on the other hand, are not considered income to the recipient nor an allowable deduction for the spouse making the payments.

Therefore, whenever a divorce occurs, it is extremely important to specifically spell out whether payments are for alimony or child support. If both are part of the divorce decree, the portion earmarked for each purpose should be clearly indicated.

SCHOOLING FOR A HANDICAPPED CHILD
Deductible, But Subject To Narrow Interpretation

The cost of schooling for a physically or mentally handicapped child or one needing psychiatric treatment is a deductible medical expense. This would seem to be a fairly straight-forward definition. Still, the Internal Revenue Service makes a critical distinction between "special" and "regular" schools.

For the educational expenses to be deductible on medical grounds, the principal function of the institution must be to treat or alleviate a handicap. While the school can also provide a normal educational curriculum, the learning must be incidental to the medical care.

Unless the school has medical treatment as its primary function, the costs are not deductible. This applies even in the case where a doctor may feel that the handicapped child would benefit from a normal school environment.

NONBUSINESS BAD DEBTS
Deductible As Short Term Capital Loss

A nonbusiness debt, as the name implies, is one which has no connection with the individual's business. Loans between friends and between family members would obviously fall in this category. If such a debt should become entirely worthless, it is treated as a short term capital loss. The key is entirely worthless. There is no deduction for partial worthlessness.

Since loans between friends and family members could be interpreted as gifts, it is essential that all actions pertaining to the loan be conducted in a businesslike fashion. That means the one making the loan should get a note specifying the amount loaned, the time for repayment and the rate of interest charged. It may be very difficult to get a deduction if the loan is granted with nothing more than a handshake.

As a short term capital loss, legitimate nonbusiness bad debts do not qualify for an unlimited tax deduction. In any one year, the maximum capital loss that can be used to offset ordinary income is $3,000. Since the nonbusiness debt is viewed as a short term capital loss, it can be deducted dollar for dollar against ordinary income, up to the $3,000 annual maximum.

INSURANCE ASSIGNMENT
Remove Insurance Proceeds From Your Estate

For anyone with a large estate, it might be a good idea to consider assigning life insurance policies to a spouse or other beneficiary. When the IRS calculates your taxable estate, insurance proceeds will be included, even if they are paid directly to a beneficiary and not to the estate. Assigning the policy is a relatively easy way to permanently remove the proceeds from your estate.

When the policy is assigned, it is essential that you surrender all rights or "incidents of ownership." This means that you must give up the power to:

- surrender or cancel the policy;
- convert from a group to an individual policy without evidence of insurability if you change jobs or get fired;
- assign or revoke a policy assignment;
- and pledge the policy as security on a loan or borrow against its cash value.

To accomplish a proper assignment of the policy, a notice of assignment must be filed with your insurance company. It must clearly stipulate that you relinquish all rights to the policy to the new owner.

If the policy has a cash value, a gift tax may be assessed. This should be considered before making the assignment.

TAX CREDIT FOR POLITICAL CONTRIBUTIONS
Credit Of Up To $100 For Joint Return

A limited credit against Federal tax is available to an individual for political contributions. The credit, equal to one-half of the contribution, is limited to $50 ($100 on a joint return). To qualify for this special credit, the contribution must be made to:

- A candidate for Federal, state or local elective office in a primary, general or special election.

- An organization or committee organized exclusively to support one or more candidates for Federal, state or local elective office.

- A national, state or local committee of a national political party.

No such credit is allowed to corporations, estates or trusts. Furthermore, the cost of raffle, lottery or similar tickets to raise campaign funds does not qualify for the credit. No charitable deduction may be taken for political contributions.

CHILD AND DEPENDENT CARE CREDIT
A Tax Break For Dependent Care If You Work

Starting with taxable year 1976, a special tax credit is allowed for 20% of all qualifying child or dependent care expenses paid for the purpose of being gainfully employed. To be eligible for the credit, the taxpayer must maintain a household for one of the following individuals:

- A dependent under age 15 for whom a dependency exemption may be claimed.

- Any dependent who is physically or mentally incapable of caring for himself and to whom the taxpayer contributes more than half of the support.

- A spouse if he or she is physically or mentally incapable of caring for himself or herself.

Qualifying expenses include those paid for household services and for the care of the qualifying individual. Services outside of the home qualify only if they involve the care of a child under age 15.

The maximum amount of employment related expenses to which the credit can be applied is $2,000 if one qualifying child or dependent is involved and $4,000 if more than one is involved. The maximum credit for one qualifying individual is $400 (20% of $2,000); the maximum credit if two or more dependents are involved is $800 (20% of $4,000).

The qualifying employment related expenses may be taken into account in determining the credit only to the extent of earned income. In the case of married taxpayers, the expenses are limited to the earned income of the spouse with the lesser income. In most cases, if one spouse is not employed, no credit is allowed unless that spouse is a full-time student.

STOCK DIVIDENDS
A Simple Way To Defer Tax Liabilities

Stock dividends provide a unique opportunity for investors who wish to accumulate capital while at the same time postpone the tax liabilities. Under normal circumstances, the recipient of a stock distribution does not incur any tax liability until the shares are eventually liquidated. When the shares are finally sold, all stock dividends are taxed at the long term capital gains rate, providing the necessary one year holding requirement is met. Cash dividends, on the other hand, are taxed as ordinary income in the year they are received (after the $100 dividend exclusion).

UNIFORMS AND SPECIAL CLOTHING
The Cost And Upkeep Of Such Apparel Is Deductible

If a uniform or other special clothing is required as a condition of employment and it is not adaptable to general wear, the cost and upkeep of such apparel are deductible. If you are reimbursed by your employer for uniform expenses, the reimbursement is included in income, but the cost is deductible from gross income. If the cost exceeds the reimbursement, any excess is deductible from adjusted gross income if deductions are itemized.

A deduction is also allowed for other special items required for employment such as work shoes and special gloves. To qualify, however, these items cannot replace items of ordinary clothing.

LOBBYING EXPENSE
Deduction Allowed For Influencing Legislation

Any taxpayer may take a business expense deduction for an ordinary and necessary expenditure related to certain types of activities aimed at promoting or combating legislation. An expense is deductible if it is paid or incurred in one of the following:

- In direct connection with an appearance before, submission of statements to, or sending communications to, a Congressional committee or legislative bodies of states or U.S. possessions in regard to legislation of direct interest to the taxpayer.

- In direct connection with communication of information between the taxpayer and a trade or business organization of which he is a member concerning legislation of direct interest to both parties.

Part of the dues for membership in an organization engaged in such activities is deductible. The deduction is limited to that portion which is attributable to the expenses incurred by the organization engaged in such activities.

Expenses incurred in an attempt to influence the general public are not deductible.

GOVERNMENT SECURITIES
Free From State And Local Taxes

Over the past several years, Government securities have become increasingly popular. Rising interest rates have clearly been the major selling point. Additionally, Government securities have enjoyed a gilt-edged rating among investors. The willingness and ability of the Federal Government to meet its obligations cannot be doubted and consequently prompt payment of both interest and principal are virtually assured.

While safety and high yield are probably the primary reasons most individuals consider Government securities, they also provide some unique tax advantages. Specifically, all Federal securities are exempt from state and local taxes. That is the extent of their tax-exempt status, however. Government bonds are subject to Federal income, estate and gift taxes. They are also subject to state and local estate and gift taxes. Still, in those states and localities which have resorted to income taxes, the savings can be significant.

BROKERAGE COMMISSIONS
Can Reduce Profit Or Increase Loss

When trading common stocks, bonds or other securities, the commissions paid to the broker are added to the cost, thus effectively raising your cost basis. For example, if an investor were to buy 100 shares of a $20 stock, the total transaction would equal

$2,000. Additionally, if $50 were paid in the form of a brokerage commission, this amount would be added to the cost of the stock. Therefore, in the future, the investor would use $2,050 as his cost basis. This effectively raises the cost basis and would serve to reduce the capital gains liability should the shares be sold at some future date for a profit.

Just as commissions are added to the cost when securities are purchased, they are subtracted from the selling price when the security is sold.

TREASURY BILLS
Attractive Yield Plus Tax Deferral

U.S. Treasury bills are short term instruments of the Federal Government. Maturity dates extend for not more than one year. Treasury bills are sold at a discount. Thus, you receive your "interest" immediately in the form of the discount. For a cash basis taxpayer, however, no tax is due until the bill is redeemed at its face value at maturity. This tax deferment is possible because of an exception to the usual rule requiring original issue discount to be "accrued" by a cash basis taypayer where the obligation doesn't run for more than one year.

This means that any taxpayer buying a Treasury bill in one year which does not mature until the next year can defer his tax liability until maturity. In addition, the interest on Treasury bills is exempt from state and local taxes.

MEDICAL DEDUCTIONS
Lump Your Deductions For Maximum Benefits

Subject to certain limitations, a taxpayer is entitled to an income tax deduction for any medical expense that is incurred in the diagnosis, treatment, cure, mitigation or prevention of a disease. The most serious of these limitations is the rule that you can only deduct those medical and dental expenses that exceed 3% of your adjusted gross income. Furthermore, drug costs over 1% of income can be deducted, as can up to $150 of annual insurance premiums. On a joint return, the 3% limitation is based on the total adjusted gross income of both husband and wife. The 3% limitation applies without regard to age.

In view of this limitation, the best way to maximize your medical deductions is to try to lump them in a single year (without endangering your health, of course). For instance, you can arrange to have your annual medical check-ups in January and December of the same year, defer payment of a medical bill, or stock up on medicines and special health foods that your doctor may have prescribed.

In addition to fees paid for the services of physicians, surgeons, psychologists and other medical experts, there are many other expenses related to health care that qualify as deductions.

You can deduct the cost of any special equipment that is prescribed by your doctor for a specific ailment. This would include wheelchairs, special beds, crutches, oxygen supplies and even prescription shoes. If the patient has recovered from an illness and no longer requires the equipment, it can be donated to a hospital and a second deduction then taken for its fair market value.

If an improvement or addition is made to your house for medical reasons on your doctor's advice, it is deductible. If the installation does not increase the value of your home, the entire cost may be deducted. Otherwise, only the excess of the cost over the increase in the home's value is allowed.

Transportation to and from your doctor's office is deductible, based on either a mileage allowance or your actual cost. If medical treatment is required in another city, the round trip cost (including meals and board while enroute) and cost of room and board in a medical facility are deductible.

LONG TERM CAPITAL GAINS
One Of The Most Popular Tax Avoidance Techniques

Down through the years, the preferential treatment afforded capital gains has been used by literally millions of Americans. Changes in the capital gains rates were one of the most controversial issues facing the 95th Congress. After considerable debate, a compromise was reached which served to liberalize the rules.

Under the old law, half of an individual's net long term gains (reduced by net short term losses, if any) could be excluded from income before applying regular tax rates (14% to 70%). This meant that the tax on gains ranged from 7% to 35%, with taxpayers in brackets above 50% given the option of having the first $50,000 in gains taxed at no more than 25%. The excluded half of capital gains, in addition, was considered an item of tax "preference" subject to existing minimum tax requirements. This could raise the maximum rate on capital gains as high as 49.125%.

The new law raises the capital gains exclusion from 50% to 60%, effective November 1, 1978. The alternative 25% rate on the first $50,000 was repealed. The excluded 60% of gains — as well as excess itemized deductions — would be subjected to a newly created alternative minimum tax. The alternative minimum tax would apply only if it exceeded regular taxes plus the existing minimum tax on preference items other than the 60% exclusion and excess itemized deductions. The new alternative tax would be applied to taxable income plus the excluded part of gains plus excess itemized deductions minus a $20,000 exemption. The rate would be 10% on the first $40,000, 20% on the next $40,000 and 25% on anything over $80,000.

The required holding period to establish a long term gain remains one year. Only long term gains enjoy preferential treatment. Short term gains, if not offset by long or short term losses, are taxed as ordinary income.

SELLING YOUR HOME
A One Time Tax Break For Selling Your House

Someone who sells a home for a profit can postpone the capital gains tax providing he buys a new one costing at least as much as the selling price within 18 months. This applies regardless of age.

There is an additional one time break for the elderly. Under the provisions of the 1978 tax bill, anyone 55 or older can take a one time exclusion of up to $100,000 profit on the sale of a home. To qualify, the individual would have to have owned and occupied the house for three of the previous five years. Furthermore, profits on home sales are exempt from the minimum tax. These provisions became effective as of July 26, 1978.

One other change pertains to so-called tax-free "rollovers" discussed above. In the past, only one such rollover could be taken every 18 months. Now, more than one is allowed if the homeowner moves for employment reasons.

TAX SHELTERS

TABLE OF CONTENTS

Tax Shelter Highlights

• Worthwhile *tax sheltered investments* offer both investment merit and tax benefits.

• "Tax shelter" means turning dollars otherwise paid to Uncle Sam into assets or income, through: (1) tax *deferral,* (2) conversion of ordinary income into long-term capital gains, and (3) conversion and deferral—the conversion of this year's ordinary income into future years' long-term capital gains.

• *Limited partnerships* are the best *tax sheltered investment* for most investors because of limited liability and flow-through of tax losses.

• As a tax shelter investor, you should have: (1) substantial net worth and assets, (2) sufficient current assets and liquidity (3) an understanding of tax shelter risk.

• The three major investment goals of tax shelter—*tax savings, tax sheltered cash flow* and *capital gains—can't all be maximized simultaneously.*

• Most tax shelters involve *public programs* organized as *limited partnerships* in: newly constructed real estate, existing income producing real estate, net leased real estate, oil and gas drilling, equipment leasing or agriculture.

• Certain investors find specialized tax shelters/Keogh Plans, individual retirement accounts, annuities, corporate pension and profit sharing plans, municipal bonds—well suited to their needs.

• Selecting a tax shelter requires analysis of your own qualifications and characteristics, your investment goals and desired results.

• Always consult your tax advisor before finalizing any tax shelter investment decision.

• A Broker maintains a separate department to analyze and evaluate prospective shelter recommendations; decisions are often verified by independent consultants.

• Your Broker will gladly review current tax shelter offerings with you and your advisor to help you determine the best course of action.

Introduction

A tax shelter is any investment made more attractive by the timing of the profit or the way it is taxed. Before we go further—please don't worry that tax shelters are somehow illegal or immoral; they aren't. And don't confuse "tax shelter" with "loophole." Tax shelters are not loopholes at all.

Tax sheltered investments are based on specific provisions of the tax laws enacted by Congress to encourage investment capital to flow directly into the basic areas of our economy such as housing, petroleum, manufacturing and agriculture. In one sense "tax shelter" means investing in vital industries in a way that permits you—rather than the companies you invest with—to keep the tax benefits . . . while retaining your opportunities for significant profits.

If you have a substantial net worth and your combined Federal and State income taxes place you in at least the 50% tax bracket, you ought to consider some of the established ways to reduce the amount you have to pay the Government on April 15th.

At our Office, we've helped many clients seek solutions to excessive tax burdens through the investment incentives contained in the tax laws and we've learned a lot that can help you.

There's a world of difference between tax advantages and the risks and rewards found in various tax shelters. Different types are best for different investors and not everyone should consider tax shelter investing. We've prepared this booklet to help you evaluate tax shelters in the context of your own financial and tax situation.

The initial section introduces the concepts. Then, we outline tax shelter INVESTMENT GOALS. The next sections deal with the MAJOR TAX SHELTERS and some SPECIALIZED TAX SHELTERS. There's also a section on the machanics of INVESTING IN TAX SHELTERS.

Finally there's a GLOSSARY covering tax shelter terms. We've prepared the glossary because it's widely held that tax shelters are very complicated. Actually, they're relatively simple; it's the *language* of tax shelters that cause problems. Some things needing explanation are taxation principles; others are part of the special vocabulary of tax sheltered investments. To simplify the explanation process, we've put the key terms in *italics* in the text and defined them in the glossary. The glossary begins on page 23.

A tax sheltered investment is the sum of two components. First and foremost, it has to be an investment with potential economic benefits. We believe any tax shelter that doesn't offer promise of being a worthwhile economic investment should be ignored. Without profit possibilities, chances are you'd do just as well at tax time giving money to a favorite charity. In addition there has to be favorable tax treatment permitting you—and other properly qualified, high tax bracket investors—to reduce or defer your overall taxes.

Viewpoint

THE TAX SHELTER INDUSTRIES

The majority of investment quality tax shelters are found in four areas:

REAL ESTATE
OIL AND GAS
EQUIPMENT LEASING
AGRICULTURE

In addition, there are several specialized tax shelter areas which may interest you: Keogh Plans, annuities, pension and profit sharing plans, individual retirement accounts and municipal bonds.

TAX SHELTER CONCEPTS

The idea behind tax shelters lies in turning dollars otherwise paid to Uncle Sam into income or into assets which may be sold for a profit. This process involves three concepts:

(1) *Deferral:* Postponing payment of taxes from the current taxable year until a later year when you're in a lower tax bracket or have more cash.

(2) *Conversion:* Obtaining current tax *deductions* against ordinary income while turning future revenues into income taxable at more favorable *capital gains* rates or lower rates derived from favorable tax features such as *depletion* or *depreciation*.

(3) *Leverage:* Obtaining current deductions in excess of cash investment through the use of loans: either *non-recourse loans* which increase *deductions* without increasing your investment or personal liability, or through *recourse loans* for which you are personally liable. Non-recourse loans currently apply only to real estate tax shelters. Since enactment of the Tax Reform Act of 1976 and the Revenue Act of 1978, recourse loans must be used fo all tax shelters other than real estate if you are to have deductions in excess of 100% of your investment.

If you have unusually high income for one year, but don't expect to be at the same level in subsequent years, you may select a tax shelter emphasizing deferral. On the other hand, if your income continually puts you in a high tax bracket, you may want a shelter which will generate deductions for several years. In both cases the use of leverage may help you increase your tax benefits.

TAX SHELTER ORGANIZATIONS

Probably the most frequent question asked by our clients about tax shelters is: "Just what is tax shelter?"

The answer: a tax shelter is a security, but not a stock, bond or commodity. What you receive when you invest in a tax shelter is an interest in a *limited partnership, joint venture* or, in rare instances, a *Subchapter S Corporation*.

LIMITED PARTNERSHIP TAX SHELTERS

To fully understand a limited partnership, you need to study its five basic features: partnership, general partner, limited partners, limited liability and flow-through of tax benefits. In addition, you should understand the difference between a "public" program and a "private" program.

THE PARTNERSHIP CONCEPT
A limited partnership is an undertaking between an individual and/or a company (called the *general partner*) that has investment expertise in a tax shelter industry and a group of investors (called *limited partners*) seeking specific tax benefits, risks and rewards. The general partner provides investment expertise; investors supply the money, or most of it. Tax benefits normally accrue to investors; profits are shared according to a stated formula designed to compensate company and investors for their respective contributions.

THE GENERAL PARTNER'S ROLE
Principal activities of the general partner include: assembling investors' capital, making investments, keeping partnership books, reporting results and distributing any partnership profits.

"Making investments" involves purchasing direct interests in oil wells, real estate, leasable equipment or various forms of agriculture on behalf of the limited partnership.

THE LIMITED PARTNER'S ROLE
Your function involves providing a share of the capital to finance initial selection and operation of partnership projects. You receive periodic progress reports and your share of partnership cash distributions. To preserve the tax status of the limited partnership, you and other limited partners must not take any active role in partnership management.

LIMITED LIABILITY
Your personal liability as a limited partner is legally limited to what you've

actually invested or committed to invest plus your share of any undistributed profits. If something goes wrong (a major fire or an earthquake for example), the partnership's creditors can't attach your personal assets except to the extent of any recourse loans for which you have agreed to become personally liable. Limited liability is the principal reason why tax shelter recommendations are concentrated on limited partnerships.

FLOW-THROUGH OF TAX BENEFITS

The partnership itself pays no taxes; benefits pass directly to the partners. You include your share of partnership profits and losses (usually losses in the early years) on your own tax return. Later, if your partnership begins generating taxable profits, those profits are added to your other income.

PUBLIC AND PRIVATE PROGRAMS

Often, the general partner's role of "assembling investor's capital" means a formal offering registered with the SEC and offered through brokers. Typically, these public programs involve a minimum $5,000 *subscription* with additional investment amounts available in *units* as small as $1,000. Assessments, if any, are limited to a stated amount or percentage of the original subscription. Public programs can be *blind pools,* an approach which gives the sponsor flexibility in selecting a diversified group of projects designed to meet partnership goals.

The substantial investor with much more income to shelter than the $5,000 minimum subscription required of most public programs may find a private program more suitable. Private offerings of tax shelters generally involve a large *subscription* with *units* of $50,000 or more. *Assessments* are more common than in public programs. The *offering amount* is typically less than $1 million; many are *specified property programs* involving one or a very few projects. If your tax advisor feels that your goals would be best met through private program investing, your broker can help you select a private program. However, you should realize that private program suitability standards are stricter than for public programs.

INVESTMENT GOALS

Before considering a *tax sheltered partnership* you should determine whether your own financial and tax position justifies such an investment. A $5,000 *minimum subscription* is required for many shelters. This amount represents a major investment decision and should be analyzed as such.

Before getting into tax shelters, you should conduct a "personal audit" to determine whether you have the prerequisites to become a tax shelter investor and, more importantly, whether you can really benefit.

PREREQUISITES

As a tax shelter investor, it's vital that you have: (1) substantial net worth and income, (2) sufficient current assets to avoid impairing other investment goals, and (3) an understanding of the risks and the lack of liquidity.

NET WORTH AND INCOME

The definition of "substantial" net worth and income varies from person to person and from tax shelter tc tax shelter; however, there are some guidelines. Many states require that prospective tax shelter investors meet "suitability requirements." For example, state regulators usually require that oil and gas investors have minumum net worth of $200,000 or net worth of $50,000 and some income taxed at a 50% rate. Tax shelters with lesser risk, i.e., equipment leasing, have correspondingly lower suitability requirements. Your broker can provide information on suitability requirements for the various types of tax shelters.

CURRENT ASSETS

Another way to analyze whether you're "suitable" is to evaluate your current assets—possible sources of tax shelter investment cash. Your investment shouldn't come out of funds earmarked for college education or retirement. And you shouldn't forgo other investments. Tax shelter funds should come out of current income, borrowings which you'll repay out of current income or current capital gains. Remember, your objective is sheltering current taxable income.

UNDERSTANDING RISK AND LIQUIDITY

The reasons for concern about current assets, income and net worth related to two characteristics of all tax shelters: investment risk and lack of liquidity.

It's difficult to quantify investment risk, but in every tax sheltered investment there's underlying danger that oil wells will be dry, that apartments won't rent, that even companies with Triple A credit can't meet lease payments or that tax laws will change. Even if you have sufficient income, net worth and available cash, you should understand that you may be faced with disappointing performance. "Investment risk" implies a range of returns—some great years, some less than great, some bad. With some tax shelters, you must be prepared to continue re-investing for enough years to average your investment performance.

An understanding of *liquidity* is also required. Whatever shelter you choose, it may be at least six months before you begin receiving any cash distributions and up to two years before you can sell out and receive the *cash liquidating value* of your chosen partnership. Don't count on being able to sell a partnership interest like a stock or a bond on a moment's notice, even in an emergency.

If you meet the suitability requirements . . . if you have capital available from proper sources . . . if you're prepared to invest in your chosen tax shelter industry long enough to smooth out the effect of investment risk . . . if you can live with the idea that it may be two years or longer before you get your money out . . . then you can probably benefit from a long-term tax shelter investment program.

POSSIBLE BENEFITS

Once you've determined that tax shelters are suitable for your portfolio, you'll have to decide what combination of the benefits offered by tax shelters fits your own investment goals: (1) tax savings, (2) tax sheltered cash flow, or (3) capital gains.

TAX SAVINGS

Reducing current taxes is the principal goal of most tax shelter investors. Limited partnerships are usually structured to maximize tax *deductions* in the first year. The objective is to have *tax losses*, i.e., a tax shelter that generates more deductions than income the first year or first few years. When combined with other income on your tax return, your share of partnership deductions offsets an equal amount of your taxable income from other sources on April 15th. If you're in a 50% Federal tax bracket, for example, each dollar of your share of net partnership deductions generates *tax savings* of up to 50¢.

Let's illustrate the effect of various degrees of deductibility in tax shelters. Assume you're in a 50% Federal tax bracket, file a joint return, have $75,000 of taxable income and invest $10,000:

Tax Deductions from Shelter in First Year as a Percentage of the Investment

	50% Deductible	100% Deductible	150% Deductible	Nothing Deductible
Taxable Income*	$75,000	$75,000	$75,000	$75,000
Deductions from Shelters	(5,000)	(10,000)	(15,000)	—
Revised Taxable Income	$70,000	$65,000	$60,000	$75,000
Tax Due	$24,700	$22,200	$19,700	$27,200
Tax Savings	$ 2,500	$ 5,000	$ 7,500	$ —
Net Investment Cost ($10,000 minus Tax Savings)	$ 7,500	$ 5,000	$ 2,500	$ —

*Personal Service income after exemptions and itemized deductions.

The 50% deduction on a $10,000 investment, for example, saves $2,500 in taxes, so the net cost is only $7,500 even though you have $10,000 invested. The 100% and 150% deductible shelters produce tax savings of $5,000 and $7,500 respectively.

Try to resist the urge to conclude that the 150% deductible tax shelter is "best" because it saves the most taxes. It may be the best if reducing current taxes is your only goal. But remember, deductions in excess of your investment are achieved only through borrowing which utilizes either *non-recourse loans* (in real estate) or *recourse loans* (all other tax shelters). You can't deduct more than your share of partnership expenses; without borrowing, your partnership can't expend more than you invest. Also remember, borrowing has to be repaid; this will involve additional risk especially if recourse loans are used. The funds used to make those repayments may increase your tax bill in later years and reduce your potential economic benefits.

TAX SHELTERED CASH FLOW

Any income received from a tax shelter partnership may be partially or wholly offset by on-going costs. Depreciation and depletion are particularly important because they are *non-cash charges*; your taxable income is reduced by the deductions, but no cash is actually paid to anyone—it's only a bookkeeping transaction. Let's look at how one dollar of tax sheltered income from a hypothetical tax sheltered investment might yield *tax sheltered cash flow*:

Joint Return—50% Tax Bracket	With Tax Shelter	Without Tax Shelter
Taxable Income*	$260,000	$260,000
60% Capital Gains Deduction	(120,000)	(120,000)
Net Taxable Income	$140,000	$140,000
100% Deductible Tax Shelter**	(80,000)	—
Revised Taxable Income	$ 60,000	$140,000
Tax Due (Including Tax Preference)	$ 32,000	$ 67,000
Tax Savings	$ 35,100	
Net Investment Cost	$ 44,900	

* Personal service net income $60,000; capital gains $200,000.
** Assumes $40,000 of tax preference items.

In this example, you receive 18¢ in cash out of each dollar of gross income generated by your tax sheltered investment. In addition, deductions reduce your taxable income from the same dollar to minus 10¢ which offsets 10¢ in taxable income from other sources and reduces your tax bill by 5¢. Because deductions offset the tax liability, you receive 18¢ of tax sheltered cash flow.

Some tax shelters yield fully tax sheltered cash flow plus additional tax losses, as in the example above. Other shelters produce some deductions but not enough to absorb all the tax liability, thus partially sheltering your cash flow received. Still other shelters generate: (1) fully taxable cash flow, (2) tax losses but no cash flow, or (3) taxable income but no cash flow received, as in some high *leverage* situations requiring large loan repayments.

Because of the necessity to repay borrowed funds, leverage will reduce the possibility of receiving cash flow. Thus, a tax shelter offering maximum first year deductions through leverage will not generally satisfy a need for tax sheltered cash flow in later years.

CAPITAL GAINS
If your partnership sells any assets, or if you sell your interest in a partnership, you have to pay a tax on your share of any profits.

If the assets sold are *capital assets*, the sale may qualify for taxation at long term *capital gains* rates rather than ordinary income tax rates. Since long term capital gains are taxed at a maximum rate of 28% against a 70% maximum rate for other types of income—capital gains may provide a significant degree of tax shelter.

Any investment plan seeking maximum tax savings in the first few years, or maximum tax sheltered cash flow in later years, may limit capital gains possibilities. Here's why: In certain instances when *accelerated depreciation* or *intangible drilling costs* have been claimed as *deductions*, a portion of those deductions are subject to *recapture* as ordinary income in the year of the sale. This feature may limit capital gains, particularly if leverage has been employed.

In summary, you won't find a tax shelter that offers maximum tax savings, maximum tax sheltered cash flow and maximum capital gains opportunities. You'll have to decide which tax shelter investment goals are best for your situation. For example, if you have a very high annual income continuing for several years, some combination of tax savings and capital gains may be your goal. On the other hand, if you're nearing retirement, you may want to forego maximum tax savings in favor of tax sheltered cash flow to augment your retirement fund; alternatively, you may decide to seek ways to defer your current taxes and pay them at your lower, post-retirement tax rate.

Whichever approach you take, the benefits from your chosen tax shelter may be lessened by certain aspects of the Tax Reform Act of 1976 and the Revenue Act of 1978. To insure that really substantial investors don't utilize tax shelters to avoid all taxes, Congress has enacted certain changes affecting the *minimum tax*, and has added a new alternative minimum tax.

Under the *minimum tax*, you pay additional income tax equal to 15% of your total *tax preference items* (except that there's no minimum tax due on the first $10,000 of tax preferences or one-half of your regular income tax, whichever is greater). There are seven tax preference items; for purposes of the regular 15% minumum tax, three relate to tax shelters: (a) *accelerated depreciation of real property and leased personal property*, (b) *depletion*, and (c) *intangible drilling costs*. (See the definition of *tax preference items* in the glossary for details.)

Maximum tax related to personal service income, i.e., what is commonly called "earned income," wages, salaries, professional fees and certain payments from pensions, annuities and deferred compensation. It is subject to a maximum tax of 50%; however, the amount of income eligible for the maximum tax is offset by the amount of the year's tax preference items. The amount offset is taxable as unearned income at rates up to 70%. Under the Revenue Act of 1978, the non-taxes portion of long-term capital gains no longer offsets the personal service income eligible for maximum tax.

However, the Revenue Act of 1978 enacted the "alternative minimum tax" to replace the exemption of capital gains and adjusted itemized deduction tax preferences from the regular 15% minimum tax. This tax, which is imposed only if it exceeds the non-corporate taxpayer's regular tax (including the regular minimum tax), is computed by adding to regular taxable income the amount of the capital gains and adjusted itemized deduction preferences.

This amount is subject to various rates, the maximum being 25% in excess of $80,000.

These three concepts are complex, but in general, the larger your taxable income and the more you invest in tax shelters, the more likely you'll be affected.

All factors should be evaluated in light of your asset base, cash position, risk tolerance and income level. Working as a team with you and your tax advisor, your broker can recommend an investment suitable for your needs.

The Major Tax Shelters

The majority of tax shelter recommendations are concentrated in the areas of real estate, oil and gas, equipment leasing and agriculture. This group offers: (1) a wide range of benefits satisfying virtually any tax shelter investment goal; (2) a broad spectrum of risk/reward relationships; (3) a variety of offerings from which to select; and, (4) well established principles of taxation.

REAL ESTATE

Real estate is undoubtedly the most popular tax shelter. Because of its similarity to home ownership, it is easily understood.

The obvious distinction between a home and investment real estate is that tenants occupy investment buildings and make periodic lease or rental payments to cover costs of operations, maintenance and debt retirement as well as profit. The not-so-obvious difference relates to taxation. Owners of investment real estate are allowed deductions for taxes, operating and maintenance expenses, interest on mortgage money and depreciation on buildings (but not land). Homeowners are allowed deductions for taxes and interest paid on mortgages, thus making home ownership probably the most widely used tax shelter. However, homeowners are denied the other deductions.

TYPES OF PROGRAMS

"Real Estate" is an umbrella term describing a variety of investments. Real estate limited partnerships involve raw land, office buildings, apartments, industrial parks, shopping centers, and mobile home parks, to name a few.

The SEC-registered real estate partnerships which most brokers recommend cluster in four areas: newly constructed real estate, existing income producing real estate, new leased real estate and government assisted housing.

Some real estate partnerships are *specified property programs*; others are *blind pool programs* involving properties selected after partnership operations begin.

Newly constructed Real Estate—These programs construct new buildings or purchase new "first user" building. Typically, newly constructed real estate programs involve maximum *leverage* and employ *accelerated depreciation*. Because of more favorable *double declining balance* depreciation (at 200% of the straight line depreciation rate), these programs usually concentrate on new apartment construction. Sometimes commercial properties (office buildings and shopping centers), which are limited to 150% declining balance depreciation, are included for diversification.

High *leverage* from *non-recourse loans* and accelerated depreciation mean tax losses of up to 50% over the first 5-10 years of the partnership.

New buildings (which might not rent easily) financed with high leverage imply high risk. Because of leverage, tax losses may continue for several years. Unusually attractive capital gains possibilities may be reduced by *recapture* of a portion of accelerated depreciation, particularly in the early years.

Interest and Taxes During Construction—The Tax Reform Act of 1976 enacted special rules regarding the deductibility of interest and taxes related to real property during construction periods. When fully operative, these rules will require that such interest and taxes be capitalized and amortized over a ten-year period thereby reducing the deductions otherwise available from real estate ventures. There are transitional rules which apply this treatment to nonresidential real estate, residential real estate, and government-subsidized housing where the construction period begins after 1975, 1977 and 1981, respectively.

Existing Income Producing Real Estate—These partnerships usually invest in existing commercial properties and apartments. Because of slower depreciation methods (125% declining balance on apartments, straight-line on commercial) and lower leverage, most existing property programs offer lower tax losses in early years (10% to 20% the first year) and significant opportunities for tax sheltered cash flow, hence the name "income producing real estate." Lower leverage on existing (hence more predictable) rental properties implies lesser risk. Established properties offer capital gains opportunities with fewer recapture problems because of lower accelerated depreciation.

Net Leased Real Estate—These partnerships purchase office buildings, hotels, shopping centers, factory buildings, warehouses and mini-warehouses, etc., on a leveraged basis. Properties are leased to major corporations on a long term, "triple net lease" basis; the corporate tenant is responsible for a specified lease payment plus all taxes, insurance, maintenance and other expenses during the life of the lease.

Tax losses the first year are minimal (remember, tenants pay operating costs; the partnership's only deductions are interest and straight-line depreciation). The real benefit in a net lease program is the opportunity for a relatively low-risk investment yielding cash flow partially tax sheltered by depreciation (usually about 50% of the cash received over the life of the partnership is tax sheltered).

Government Assisted Housing—These investments depend upon funding from various state and federal housing finance programs; therefore, they are not always available. All involve construction or rehabilitation of properties for low income, middle income or elderly tenants. Accelerated depreciation plus extreme leverage (made possible by government loan guarantees and/or rent subsidies) create excellent tax loss possibilities, up to 200% the first year. Leverage and provisions of some Federal laws may limit tax sheltered cash flow; however, there will be a continuing stream of tax losses for several years. Recapture provisions severely reduce possibilities for early capital gains.

REAL ESTATE PARTNERSHIP OPERATIONS
All real estate limited partnerships function similarly—only the properties purchased and the tax treatment vary. Typically the general partner is a real estate developer, property management company or real estate broker. The general partner subtracts a *management fee* and *organization and offering expenses.* Then he applies partnership *proceeds* to a group of properties which meet stated partnership objectives. First year tax losses are derived from partnership and property operating expenses, depreciation, and interest deductions, etc.

After partnership properties are in operation, rental income is designated for property management, maintenance and repayment of loans. (In partnership involving net leases, the tenants pay all expenses except loan repayment.) Any excess is divided among the general and limited partners according to an established formula. Some general partners also receive compensation from brokerage commissions or property management fees.

OIL AND GAS
Oil and gas accumulate in pore spaces of underground rock formations. A given "reservoir," as these accumulations are called, may be small or may contain millions of barrels of oil or billions of cubic feet of natural gas.

Because of the technology required, and because of "dry holes," the search for oil and gas is expensive. Industry statistics indicate that only about one exploratory well in ten finds a new field and only one out of 40 or 50 is a significant commercial success. Because of high costs and risks, oil and gas companies are often forced to look outside for cash to finance drilling. Individual investors supply much of this drilling capital through tax shelter limited partnerships.

Oil and gas investment represents perhaps the best all-around tax shelter. It offers opportunities for high first year tax losses, partially tax sheltered cash flow and capital gains. Oil and gas is also the riskiest tax shelter because of "dry holes." However, diversifying partnership proceeds among numerous wells spreads the risk.

TYPES OF PROGRAMS
Limited partnerships that drill for oil and gas may be blind pool programs or specified property programs. Blind pools are most popular. Drilling programs are further classified according to risk. A few drill only exploratory or "wildcat wells." The majority seek to diversify risk by combining wildcats with 10% to 75% "development wells"—the wells which must be drilled over the extent of the reservoir before it can produce its maximum yield. Development drilling is considerably less risky. Roughly eight out of ten are completed as producers according to industry statistics; however, remember that a successful well may not be a profitable well. Development well sites result from someone's wildcat discovery. As you might suspect, they are expensive, limiting potential profitability of a balanced drilling partnership while lessening the risk.

General and administrative expenses, offering expenses and *intangible drilling costs* combine to offer first year tax losses of 70% to 90% of the amount invested. In one type of drilling program, the general partner pays all nondeductible costs, making 100% of your investment deductible.

Once successful wells are on stream, depletion partially shelters oil and gas gross income. You can deduct up to 22% of your share of this gross oil and gas income limited to the lesser of 65% of the partner's taxable income before the depletion allowance or 50% of the taxable income from each property in the partnership before the depletion allowance . . . as long as the wells produce. This percentage will decrease from 22% to 15% between 1980 and 1984.

Capital gains opportunities, reduced by *recapture* of a portion of *intangible drilling costs*, arise if the general partner exchanges partnership interests for common stock and you sell your stock profitably, or he offers a *cash liquidating value* which you accept.

DRILLING PROGRAM OPERATIONS
Drilling partnership general partners are normally oil and gas producers seeking investors' capital to finance operations. After deducting the *front end load*, the general partner typically drills as many wells as possible with available *proceeds*. While selecting wells which meet partnership objectives, he usually seeks diversification of risk, depth and geological area. During drilling, progress reports are distributed frequently. After drilling is complete, any income

is apportioned between the general partner and the investors (quarterly in most cases), according to an established formula.

EQUIPMENT LEASING

For industrial corporations, equipment leasing spreads large cash outlays over several years. In some instances, a lease may be classified as "off-the-balance-sheet" financing that does not hurt the corporation's borrowing capacity.

Virtually any industrial equipment can be leased: airplanes, computers, trucks, drilling rigs, entire factories, and railroad cars are examples.

Equipment leasing partnerships all require: (1) investors to provide equity capital, (2) sponsors to supervise partnership operations, (3) lenders (banks or insurance companies) to provide loans, (4) users, and (5) leasable equipment.

Equipment leasing offers a lesser risk approach to tax shelter. However, don't conclude that equipment leasing is riskless. The risk of user failure is always present; even companies with top credit ratings sometimes can't meet obligations. Another risk is obsolescence. Tax laws require that a lease must have a shorter term than the equipment's useful life if certain tax benefits are to be retained. Thus, investors bear the risk of re-leasing or selling—even if technology has rendered the equipment obsolete. Also, upon successful sale, *recapture* of certain deductions may offset gains significantly.

TYPES OF PROGRAMS

The common type of equipment leasing partnership offers deferral opportunities. Early year tax losses result from *leverage* and *accelerated depreciation* (double declining balance on new equipment or 150% declining balance on used equipment). Also, some equipment, a computer for example, has a very short useful life. "Useful life" is a tax concept related to depreciation. It may not coincide with the actual time equipment is used. For example, owners of railroad cars may elect to depreciate their equipment over a twelve year useful life even though the equipment may actually operate for several decades.

Accelerated depreciation and short useful life mean very high deductions in early years converting to taxabale income when depreciatin is exhausted—thereby deferring taxable income. Continuous re-investment over several years creates an on-going deferral of taxable income.

LEASING PARTNERSHIP OPERATIONS

The general partner typically deducts a management fee and offering expenses. Equipment is purchased using partnership proceeds and loans. The general partner typically receives a small portion of the lease payments plus a share of any equipment-sale proceeds; he may earn additional compensation by providing equimpent maintenance for users. In equipment leasing partner-ships, the general partner is usually a company that specializes in equipment leasing.

AGRICULTURE

Agricultural tax shelters include cattle feeding, cattle and other livestock breeding, crops and timber. With the exception of cattle feeding and breeding, none are widely available as *public programs*.

CATTLE FEEDING

Young "feeder cattle" are purchased with partnership *proceeds*. These cattle become collateral for recourse loans to purchase more cattle and grain for the feeding period. Interest and feed costs push total first year deductions to 50% to 100%. When "finished cattle" are sold after 4 to 6 months, bank loans are repaid and the general partner's share is deducted. Any balance is ordinary in-come to the limited partners.

Because the holding period for cattle is 24 months, there are no capital gains. Disease and price fluctuations are major risks. Risks, however, can be partially offset, but not eliminated, with hedging and insurance.

BREEDING PROGRAMS

In addition to cattle, "breeding" refers to fur-bearing animals, other farm animals and fish or shellfish. Although the "livestock" varies, program opera-tions are similar. An initial "herd" is purchased. First year tax losses can equal up to 50% to 90%; feed costs and depreciation are the principal deductions. Depreciation and investment tax credit is available on the initial herd but not on offspring.

Sale of offspring generates income. Except for fish and shellfish programs, most females and superior males are retained to increase herd size and quali-ty. Capital gains are available on livestock held more than 12 months (24 months for horses and cattle). Disease and price fluctuations are major risks. *Recapture* may reduce profitability.

CROPS

The list of potential crop partnerships covers virtually anything grown in an or-chard, field, grove or vineyard: fruits, nuts, grains, vegetables, etc. Wine grapes, nuts and citrus are the most popular program types.

Labor costs, interest and operating expenses are deductible. By using leverage, first year tax losses may approach 50% to 90%. Crop sales generate ordinary income. Depreciation may offer partially tax sheltered cash flow. Risks depend on weather, price fluctuations and whether new or mature pro-perties are involved. Capital gains, subject to recapture restrictions, are primary investment objectives when the land on which the crops are grown is finally sold.

SUMMARY

Most investors satisfy their tax shelter investment objectives through public or private programs organized as limited partnerships in newly constructed real estate, existing income producing real estate, net leased real estate, government assisted housing, oil and gas drilling, equipment leasing or agriculture.

Each major tax shelter offers a specific package of possible tax and investment benefits. In addition, each shelter investment involves risk. Although some are riskier than others, there is always the danger that your rate of return from a given investment will be less than you anticipated or, in some instances, that you may suffer total loss. Always keep risk in mind as you consult your tax advisor about possible benefits.

Specialized Tax Shelters

In addition to the real estate, oil and gas, equipment leasing and agriculture tax shelters, there are a number of personal and corporate investment vehicles which may apply to your financial situation. Your broker can supply details of Keogh Plans, annuities, pension and profit sharing plans, individual retirement accounts, and municipal bonds. None of these tax shelters utilizes the limited partnership format.

KEOGH PLANS

If you're self employed, depending on your income level, a defined contribution Keogh Plan can help you set aside between $750 and $7,500 each year tax-free for your retirement. A defined benefit Keogh Plan, when permissible in certain cases, may result in higher allowable contributions. Contributions to a Keogh Plan may be invested in a variety of investments: stock, bonds, mutual funds, etc.; all growth and income accumulate tax free. After retirement, you pay tax on the money as you withdraw it from the Plan.

ANNUITIES

An annuity is simply a contractual agreement between you and an insurance company that provides you with a very safe tax-advantaged accumulation vehicle. You pay no Federal or State income tax on the earnings while they accumulate. You never have to worry about market fluctuations since both your principal and interest are 100% guaranteed by a major insurance company. Interest is credited daily, compounded automatically at competitive secure-dollar investment rates. You can withdraw money at any time and under specified conditions, without a penalty.

At retirement, you can chose an option that will provide you with income for a specified period of years . . . for life . . . beneficiary payments upon death . . . or income for your life and your spouse's life. The monthly payments you receive are partially tax sheltered because they represent, to a degree, return of your initial deposit. In addition, the interest portion of each monthly payment is taxable at your lower, post-retirement tax rate.

PENSION AND PROFIT SHARING PLANS

Since enactment of the Employee Retirement Income Security Act of 1974 (ERISA), professionals (doctors, lawyers, accountants, architects, etc.) who incorporate can set up profit sharing plans: generally up to 15% of the annual compensation paid each participant (limited to a maximum of $32,700 in 1979 and adjusted in later years by a cost-of-living adjustment factor) may be paid out free of corporate income tax, are limited based on an actuarial funding formula compensation. Incorporated professionals may also establish pension plan contributions which are tax deductible. As in Keogh Plans, all growth and income accumulate tax free.

INDIVIDUAL RETIREMENT ACCOUNTS

ERISA also established a retirement plan for employed individuals. Any employee who is not participating in a qualified pension plan can establish his own "Individual Retirement Account." Up to $1,500 of 15% of annual compensation (whichever is smaller) may be invested in an IRA each year. A married employee with a non-working spouse can establish a joint IRA; contributions are limited to the lesser of $1,750 or 15% of compensation. If both spouses work, each can establish an IRA; the $1,500/15% limitation applies to each. All interest and appreciation in an IRA accumulate tax free. No withdrawals are permitted before age 59½; withdrawals must begin by age 70½. Withdrawals are taxed as ordinary income as received (at the lower post-retirement tax rate).

MUNICIPAL BONDS

Debt securities of states, cities and special purpose "authorities" (turnpikes, sewer and water districts, etc.) pay interest that is free of Federal and some State taxes. There are no tax losses, but 100% of the income is tax free: fully tax sheltered cash flow. Municipal bonds may be purchased directly or by investing in one of several municipal bond trusts or municipal bond mutual funds which pool the funds of several investors and purchase diversified portfolios of bonds.

Investing in Tax Shelters

To review: Most tax shelter programs are usually *limited partnerships* organized as *public programs* registered with the SEC. Most investors will select a real estate, oil and gas, or equipment leasing. Others may choose agriculture tax shelters or one of several specialized tax shelters.

SELECTING THE INDUSTRY

Unfortunately, there are no hard and fast industry-selection rules. Your situation, which is different from the next person's, changes each year. This year's tax-shelter need—maximum tax losses, maximum tax sheltered cash flow or maximum capital gains—will depend on your individual package of assets, liabilities and lifestyle plus your present and future income.

The key lies in understanding your characteristics as an investor. The tax and investment features of all shelters are well documented and widely understood. Once your characteristics are known, industry-selection becomes almost routine.

SELECTING THE PROGRAM

Analyzing any program requires in-depth knowledge of partnership law, taxation, the industry and the general partner's management and operations.

At our Company we rely on our Tax Shelter Department to screen, analyze and investigate each prospective tax shelter recommendation. We often employ independent consultants with specific industry expertise to verify our findings before we make a final decision.

Some tenets of tax shelter philosophy that guide decision making include:

Diversification—Pooling capital of several investors and spreading risk among several projects is a key benefit of limited partnerships.

Program Size—Too small a program may offer only limited diversification, or it may be excessively burdened by *front-end load*. Too large a program may force the sponsor into unwise decisions if he is under pressure to complete partnership projects before year-end.

Management—Decisions are based on integrity, past performance, experience, experience with comparable-size programs and quality of investor communications.

Sharing Arrangement—The general partner's compensation should encourage superior performance. Compensation should be derived from operating profits, not front-end fees.

Tax Features—Well accepted taxation principles avoid unnecessary "tax-risk." Programs promising excessive deductions or unreasonable expectation of investment returns are avoided.

Liquidity—Any liquidity is better than none; however, all tax shelters are, at best, illiquid. Emphasis is placed on the general partner's financial ability to provide liquidity at the appropriate time.

INVESTMENT APPLICATIONS

An integral part of selecting the "right" industry and "right" program is what you hope to accomplish by making the investment. Applications of tax sheltered investments include: (1) saving taxes by sheltering high-level, recurring income, (2) reducing tax effects of major capital gains, (3) building retirement income, (4) increasing charitable contributions, (5) employing sophisticated estate planning tactics, and (6) enhancing corporate tax planning.

RECURRING INCOME

The most familiar use of tax shelters is related to softening the burden of taxes on high-level, recurring income. If you're a high-salaried corporate executive, doctor or lawyer, for example, you pretty well know that, short of some unpredictable economic or personal calamity, you'll earn at least X dollars each year for the next Y years. You can use this knowledge and apply tax shelters to help offset your annual tax liability.

Let's assume that each year for the next ten years, you'll file a joint return with $75,000 taxable income (after exemptions and itemized deductions). Also, assume you'll make a 100% deductible, $10,000 annual tax shelter investment and you are in the 50% Federal tax bracket.

Over a ten-year period, you'll invest $100,000, but because of tax savings you'll be out of pocket only $50,000. You'll have accomplished four things: (1) reduced your annual tax bill by $5,000, (2) invested $100,000 at an out-of-pocket cost of only $50,000, (3) purchased assets which can yield an investment return with dollars that normally go to pay taxes, and (4) spread your risk.

CAPITAL GAINS

Let's suppose that in one year you have, in addition to your $60,000 recurring taxable income, a $200,000 capital gain. A good rule of thumb is to consider investing 40% of a large capital gain in a tax shelter, in this case $80,000.

This technique: (1) puts $80,000 to work for a net cost of 56¢ on the dollar, (2) reduces your tax bill 52%, and (3) still leaves you at least $120,000 cash remaining for your capital gain . . . a very powerful tax and investment planning tool.

Note: The alternative minimum tax is used in the computation of the With Tax Shelter example.

165

Joint Return-50% Tax Bracket	Cash Flow	Tax Flow
Tax Shelter Gross Income	$1.00	$1.00
Operating Expenses	(.46)	(.46)
Operating Income	$.54	$.54
Deductions:		
Depreciation (Non-cash)	—	(.34)
Interest Payments	(.30)	(.30)
Principal Payments	(.06)	—
Cash Flow Received	$ .18	
Taxable Income (Loss)		$(.10)

RETIREMENT PLANNING

If you're a few years from retirement, tax shelters—particularly those with a deferral feature—can help you take advantage of needed tax savings up to your retirement date. After retirement your tax shelter may yield ordinary income which will be taxed at your lower post-retirement tax rate.

CHARITY CONTRIBUTIONS

You invest in a tax shelter limited partnership and hold it until the cash liquidating value or other fair market value is determined. Tax laws permit a deduction up to the fair market value of an asset contributed to a qualified charitable organization. Using this technique, you have the opportunity—assuming a successful tax shelter investment—to take two deductions on the same dollars: first when you invest, then when you contribute. Your charity receives an income producing asset free of any administrative responsibilities. Note, however, that charity giving is a very sensitive tax area requiring advance consultation with both your tax advisor and your charity.

ESTATE PLANNING

The same invest-hold-contribute technique used for charity giving can be used to transfer tax shelter assets out of your estate to your children. This technique: (1) decreases your taxable estate and, ultimately, reduces inheritance taxes; also, it (2) reduced overall family tax liability by shifting your high-bracket taxable income into your children's lower tax bracket. Like charity contributions, estate planning requires careful study by your tax advisor.

CORPORATE TAX PLANNING

Corporations—particularly closely-held entities—can employ tax shelters a number of creative ways, including: (1) sheltering recurring income; (2) utiliz-

165

ing tax benefits, then contributing the investment to employee pension and profit sharing plans; (3) avoiding the penalty tax on accumulated earnings; (4) providing executive compensation through tax shelter investment loan plans.

The tax shelter process requires that you first become familiar with what your own tax shelter investment applications should be. This will help you and your tax advisor determine the application, industry and, finally, the specific program offering you the best course of action.

INVESTMENT RETURNS

Because of risk, it is impossible to say what rate of return you may receive from a given tax shelter program; losses or less-than-anticipated returns are always possible. However, with tax savings (which reduce your initial out-of-pocket investment costs), proper diversification, a proven management team and, when feasible, a three to five year program of recurring investments, risks are significantly reduced.

As soon as possible, your general partner will begin distributing your share of any partnership profits—usually within six months to two years of the date you invest (longer when a highly leveraged partnership repays bank debt). After distibutions begin, you'll probably continue receiving them on a fairly regular basis; quarterly is the most common distribution pattern.

SUMMARY

The theme of this booklet is that you shouldn't try to make tax shelter decisions alone; the subject is too complex. We suggest that you seek the counsel of your tax advisor. He can help you decide what your tax shelter needs are. Many brokers attach such great importance to tax shelters that they have created a separate department which devotes its attention exclusively to seeking, evaluating and marketing programs which offer attractive tax features and the opportunity for significant investment returns.

The person to consult for detailed information is your Broker. His Tax Sheltered Investment Department keeps him fully informed about program availability as well as those which will be coming to market in the future. He'll also provide any assistance needed in selecting the best program for your individual requirements.

Glossary goes to pg. 174

Note: terms in *italics* are defined elsewhere in the glossary.

Accelerated Depreciation—Any method of *depreciation* which permits *deduction* of a greater percentage of the cost of an asset in early years of the asset's useful life with smaller deductions in later years. Two methods are widely used: (1) the "sum-of-the-years-digits" method and (2) the more popular "declining balance" method. Under the declining balance, annual deductions are calculated as a percentage of the *straight line depreciation* rate, i.e., 200% declining balance (also called "double declining balance") available for new residential construction; 150% declining balance, availabale for new commercial construction; 125% declining balance for existing improved real estate. Note that accelerated depreciation is usually a *tax preference item*.

Assessment—Additional amounts of money which a *limited partner* in a *tax sheltered partnership* may be required to furnish beyond his original *subscription*. A given program, depending on the terms, may be either "assessable" or "non-assessable." An assessable program may have limited or unlimited assessments. Assessments may be optional or mandatory.

"At-Risk" Limitations—This limitation is designed to prevent non-corporate taxpayers from deducting losses in excess of their economic investment in the activity involved. These rules now apply to all activities except real estate and certain companies leasing equipment. In addition, where your amount of investment deemed to be "at risk" is reduced below zero (by distibutions or change of status of liabilities from recourse to non-recourse), income recognition may be required of deductions previously taken.

Blind Pool Program—A *tax sheltered partnership* which, at the time sale of *subscriptions* begins, does not have the *proceeds of the offering allocated to specific projects or properties. (Contrast with specified property program.)*

Capital Asset—Any asset (property, equipment, livestock, etc.) which is: (1) used in a trade or business (except inventories or items held for sale to customers), (2) held for production of income, or (3) given the effect of a capital asset by a tax law provision. With certain exceptions, capital assets—including interests in *tax shelter partnerships*—are subject to *capital gains* treatment on any profit (or loss) arising from sale or exchange.

Capital Gains—Usually gain (or loss) from sale or exchange of any property is included in income and taxed at ordinary income tax rates. However, if the gain is from the sale or exchange of a *capital asset* owned for more than 12 months, the tax is calculated at the lower long term capital gains rate, generally no more than 28%. Almost all types of *tax sheltered investments* except cattle feeding and equipment leasing offer some capital gains opportunities. Certain types of real estate, and oil and gas offer the most potential. It has been said that capital gains offer the major source of tax relief. Note however that capital gains benefits may be reduced by *recapture*. Note also that 60% of long-term capital gains may be taxed under the alternative minimum tax.

Cash Liquidating Value—The amount, generally based on an evaluation of a qualified independent appraiser, which will be paid by the *general partner* for an interest in a *tax sheltered partnership* upon exercise by a *limited partner* of his right to receive such value. Programs that offer cash liquidation can be described as offering "liquidity," as opposed to illiquid programs which do not have cash liquidating features.

Conversion—Obtaining current tax *deductions* against ordinary income while turning future revenues into income taxable at more favorable *capital gains* rates or lower rates derived from favorable tax features such as *depletion* or *depreciation*.

Deductions—In this context, the interest, taxes, *depreciation, depletion* and other expenses incurred in the trade or business of a *tax sheltered partnership* which are passed on to the *limited partners* thereby reducing their taxable income and, ultimately, their tax liability. The "ordinary and necessary" expenses of any business are allowable as deductions; however, certain forms of *tax sheltered intangible drilling costs* associated oil and gas, (2) depreciation and interest costs associated with real estate, equipment leasing and certain agricultural tax shelters, particularly when *leverage* is employed, and (3) the feed and maintenance costs associated with cattle feeding. Ideally, a *tax sheltered partnership* will generate deductions in excess of income for the first year or first few years thereby permitting program *limited partners* to recover part or all of their investments out of *tax losses.*

Deferral—In this context, a form of tax shelter that results from an investment timed so that *deductions* take place during the investor's high income years and taxable income is realized after retirement, in some other period of reduced income, or at a time when the tax will be more convenient to pay. Equipment leasing and certain types of real estate offer the best deferral opportunities.

Depletion—A form of *deduction* that applies to "wasting asset" interest. The purpose is to encourage exploration for new deposits by permitting recovery of exploration and development costs out of tax savings. The annual depletion deduction for any mineral property is the greater of "cost depletion" (based on the ratio of annual production to remaining reserves) and "percentage depletion" (a fixed annual lpercent). The major advantage of percentage depletion is that benefits are available each year a property produces income and do not cease when the cost of the property has been recovered. Oil and gas, timber and minerals all offer some depletion. Percentage depletion on oil and gas is 22% of gross income from each property limited to the lesser of 65% of the individual's taxable income or 50% of the taxable income from the property. However, beginning in 1981, this percentage decreases down to 15% ratably from 1981-1984. Percentage depletion on other minerals ranges from 22% for sulphur down to 5% for clay and shale. Note that percentage depletion is a *tax preference item.*

Depreciation—A form of *deduction* to permit recovery of the cost (less any salvage value) of an asset in the form of tax savings. This cost recovery is spread over the asset's "useful life" as an annual deduction from taxable income. Depreciation is most attractive in real estate, equipment leasing and some types of cattle breeding, especially if *leverage* is employed. Tax laws permit choosing a constant annual depreciation amount over useful life (called straight-line depreciation) or, in some cases, one of several *accelerated depreciation* methods.

Double Declining Balance—See: *accelerated depreciation.*

Front End Load—A slang term for the total of *organizational and offering expenses* plus *management fees:* i.e., the total deductions from the *offering amount* to arrive at the *proceeds* of a *tax sheltered partnership.* (See also: *management fees.*(

General Partner—In this context, the manager or sponsor of a *tax sheltered investment* which has been organized as a *limited partnership.* (See *limited partnership* for details.)

Intangible Drilling Costs—A tax *deduction* for certain expentitures incurred in drilling and completing oil and gas wells.

Intangibles'' are the items which have no salvage value (commonly non-material costs such as labor, chemicals, drill-site preparation, etc.). Intangibles frequently account for 50% to 80% of the cost of drilling and completing a given well. Note that intangible drilling costs on producing wells in excess of oil and gas net income is a *tax preference item.*

Joint Venture—A form of business organization. In this context, a *tax sheltered investment* in which the manager and the investors share jointly in the ownership, management authority and liability. (Contrast with *limited partnership.*)

Leverage—In this context, a method of increasing a tax shelter through borrowing (see *non-recourse loans* and *recourse loans*) as a part of a *tax sheltered investment.* The investor (in certain circumstances) is permitted *deductions* for interest, *management fees, depreciation,* etc., on the amount he invests plus his pro-rata share of the amount the partnership borrows on a non-recourse basis. Any properly-structured loans, therefore, serve to increase total deductions from income for tax purposes. Real estate offers excellent leverage possibilities, as do cattle breeding and equipment leasing.

Limited Partner—In this context, the purchaser of a *subscription* in a *tax sheltered investment* which has been organized as a *limited partnership;* i.e., an investor.

169

Limited Partnership—A form of business organization in which some partners exchange their right to participate in management for a limitation on their liability for partnership losses. Commonly, *limited partners* have liability only to the extent of their investment in the business plus their share of any undistributed profits. To establish limited liability, there must be at least one *general partner* who is fully liable for all claims against the business. Limited partnerships are a popular organizational form for *tax sheltered investments* because of the ease with which tax benefits flow through the partnership to the individual partners. (Contrast with *joint venture.*)

Liquidity—See: *cash liquidating value.*

Management Fee—An amount paid to the *general partner* of a tax sheltered partnership to cover *organization and offering expenses* and/or to repay costs of operating and administrating the partnership, commonly expressed as a percentage of the total *offering amount.*

Liquidity—See: *cash liquidating value.*

Management Fee—An amount paid to the *general partner* of a tax sheltered partnership to cover *organization and offering expenses* and/or to repay costs of operating and administrating the partnership, commonly expressed as a *percentage of the total offering amount.* Prior to the Tax Reform Act of 1976, the management fee was claimed as a *deduction* by many limited partnerships. Under present law, only the general partner's reimbursements to cover costs of operating and adminstrating the partnership are considered fully deductible. (See also: *front-end load.*)

Maximum Tax—Individuals are taxed at a maximum rate of 50% on that portion of their taxable income attributable to personal service income. However, the amount of income eligible for the maximum rate is offset by the amount the year's *tax preference items.* The amount offset is taxable as unearned income at rates of up to 70%.

Minimum Subscription—The smallest dollar amount which an investor must initially commit in order to become a *limited partner* in a *tax sheltered partnership,* usually one or more *units.* In a *public program* the minimum subscription is generally almost always $5,000. (See also: *subscription.*)

Minimum Tax—15% of total tax preference items which exceed the greater of $10,000 or one-half the taxpayer's regular Federal income tax liability. (See also: *tax preference items.*)

Alternative Minimum Tax—A tax on regular taxable income plus the long-term capital gain preference (60% untaxed portion) plus adjusted itemized deductions in excess of 60% of adjusted gross income. The resulting "alternative minimum taxable income," after a specific exemption of $20,000, is subject to the following rates of tax: 10% on the first $40,000; 20% on the next $40,000 and 25% of any excess. This tax replaces the regular tax (including the 15% minumum tax) if it exceeds that tax.

Non-Cash Charges—*Deductions* for *depreciation and depletion* which aren't actually paid to anyone, yet are subtracted from taxable income before calculating tax due. *Tax sheltered partnerships* such as real estate and equipment leasing which employ *leverage* may be able to pyramid non-cash charges to the point that limited partners receive *tax sheltered cash flow* in the early years against which there is limited or no tax liability.

Non-Recourse Loan—In this context, any borrowing by a *tax sheltered partnership,* structured in such a way that lenders can look only to specific assets pledged for repayment and not to the individual assets of the various partners. However, in the event of a foreclosure, if partnership cash and assets aren't sufficient to repay the loan balance, the limited partners may be left with a substantial tax bill because of "forgiveness of debt." Real estate is the only tax shelter area where non-recourse financing is permitted. (Contrast with *recourse loan;* see also: *leverage.*)

Offering Amount—The total dollar amount sought by a *general partner* from prospective *limited partners in a particular tax sheltered partnership.*

Organization and Offering Expenses—Those expenses incurred in connection with preparing a *tax sheltered partnership* for registration with Federal and/or state securities agencies and subsequently selling subscriptions to limited partners. Organizational and offering expenses typically include legal fees, printing costs, registration fees, sales commissions and selling costs. (See also: *Management fee; front-end load.*)

Private Program—A *tax sheltered partnership* which is offered and sold pursuant to the private offering exemption available under the Securities Act of 1933 and/or some registration exemption allowed under the securities laws of one or more states; i.e., a program which is not registered with the Securities and Exchange Commission. (Contrast with *public program.*)

Proceeds—The dollar amount remaining for the general partner to conduct partnership operations after deduction of *organization and operating expenses* or other items of *front-end load* from the total amount committed.

Public Program—A *tax sheltered partnership* whch is registered with the Securities and Exchange Commission (SEC) and distributed in a public offering by broker dealers and/or employees of the *general partner.* The principal differences between a public program and a *private program* relate to: (1) the number of *investors,* which may be several hundred in a public program, but which is limited, with certain exceptions, to 35 in a private program; (2) minimum subscription; $5,000 in a public program, $50,000 or more in a private program; and (3) the fact that "private" investors are subject to stricter suitability standards.

Recapture—Upon profitable sale of certain assets, capital gains may be severely restricted when previously claimed deductions for depreciations, farming losses, intangible drilling costs or investment credit are taken back into ordinary income (i.e., "recaptured"). Since ordinary income tax rates can run as high at 70%—versus 28% for captial gains—recapture can severely reduce or eliminate capital gains benefits. The amount of recapture depends on the type of asset, holding period, type of depreciation (straight-line or accelerated) as well as dollar amount of gain versus the amount of "recaptured" deductions.

Recourse Loan—In this context, any borrowing by a tax shelter investor for which he is personally liable. (Contrast with non-recourse loan.)

Specified Property Program—A tax sheltered partnership which, at the time sale of subscriptions begins, has the proceeds of the offering allocated to definite projects or properties which are described in detail in the prospectus or offering circular. (Contrast with blind pool program.)

Straight Line Depreciation—See: depreciation.

Subchapter S Corporation—A form of corporation with a limited number of qualified stockholders who elect to utilize a specific tax law provision which permits them to be taxed so the corporation pays no taxes and each stockholder reports his share of the corporate income (or loss) on his own tax return. (Also called a "Tax Option Corporation.")

Subscription—The total dollar amount for which a limited partner in a tax sheltered partnership initially commits. Legally it represents the amount he is obligated to pay, exclusive of any assessment amount which he has the option to reject. (See also: unit.)

Tax Loss—A situation that occurs when the deductions generated by a tax sheltered partnership exceed program revenues. Thus, the limited partner's taxable income is lower, resulting in a tax saving. Ideally, a tax sheltered partnership will generated enough tax losses the first year or first few years to permit the limited partners to recover their investment from "tax savings." However, recapture may ultimately limit these benefits.

Tax Preference Items—Items of tax preference subject to the 15% minimum tax include: accelerated depreciation in excess of straight line depreciation on real property and leased personal property, appreciation on certain stock options, excess intangible drilling costs on productive wells and excess percentage depletion.

Tax Savings—See: *tax losses.*

Tax Sheltered Cash Flow—The situation that arises when *non-cash charges* and other *deductions* exceed gross income from a tax shelter partnership so that the program has cash to distribute to *limited partners* even though the cash they may receive involves no current tax liability or is taxed at a lower rate. Real estate and equipment leasing programs employing *accelerated depreciation* and leverage are the best sources of tax sheltered cash flow.

Tax Sheltered Investment—An investment that has a expectation of economic profit, made even more attractive because of the timing of the profit or the way it is taxed, generally having some or all of the following characteristics:
(a) *Deferral* of taxes,
(b) Conversion of *deductions* to future *capital gains,*
(c) *Leverage.*
The flow-through of tax benefits is a material factor whether the entity is organized as a *limited partnership, joint venture* or *Subchapter S Corporation* and whether it is offered to investors as a *private program* or a *public program.* Common forms of tax sheltered investments include: real estate, oil and gas, equipment leasing and agriculture.

Tax Sheltered Partnership—A *tax sheltered investment* organized as a *limited partnership.* Commonly, a tax sheltered program is created to mutually benefit a *general partner* and a group of *limited partners.* It may be organized as a *public program* or a *private program.*

Unit—The smallest dollar amount into which *subscriptions* in a *tax shelter partnership* may be divided, usually $1,000 or $5,000. For example, a $1 million *public program* might consist of 200 units of $5,000 each. Alternately, it might consist of 1,000 units of $1,000 each. Each type would normally have a *minimum subscription* of $5,000.

This booklet has been prepared for informational purposed only and is not an offer to sell or the solicitation of an offer to buy any tax sheltered investment or any other security.

The material contained in this description of tax sheltered investments is based upon the provisions of the Internal Revenue Code of 1954, as presently amended, the existing applicable regulations and current administrative rulings and practice. However, it is emphasized that no assurance can be given that legislative or administrative changes will not be forthcoming which would modify this description. Any such changes may or may not be retroactive with respect to transactions entered into prior to the effective date of such changes.

Investment in tax shelters may give rise to liability for state income, property or inheritance taxes which are not discussed herein and may create the necessity for ancillary probate proceedings. Due to the complex tax and other legal considerations surrounding an investment in a tax shelter, each prospective investor is urged to consult with his own council before obligating himself to purchase an interest in a tax shelter.

ρ.175

MARRIED TAXPAYERS FILING JOINT RETURNS AND SURVIVING SPOUSES

If taxable income is:	The tax is:
Not over $3,400	No tax.
Over $3,400 but not over $5,500	14% of excess over $3,400.
Over $5,500 but not over $7,600	$294, plus 16% of excess over $5,500.
Over $7,600 but not over $11,900	$630, plus 18% of excess over $7,600
Over $11,900 but not over $16,000	$1,404, plus 21% of excess over $11,900
Over $16,000 but not over $20,200	$2,265, plus 24% of excess over $16,000.
Over $20,200 but not over $24,600	$3,273, plus 28% of excess over $20,200.
Over $24,600 but not over $29,900	$4,505, plus 32% of excess over $24,600.
Over $29,900 but not over $35,200	$6,201, plus 37% of excess over $29,900.
Over $35,200 but not over $45,800	$8,162, plus 43% of excess over $35,200.
Over $45,800 but not over $60,000	$12,720, plus 49% of excess over $45,800.
Over $60,000 but not over $85,600	$19,678, plus 54% of excess over $60,000.
Over $85,600 but not over $109,400	$33,502, plus 59% of excess over $85,600.
Over $109,400 but not over $162,400	$47,544, plus 64% of excess over $109,400.
Over $162,400 but not over $215,400	$81,464, plus 68% of excess over $162,400.
Over $215,400	$117,504, plus 70% of excess over $215,400.

UNMARRIED INDIVIDUALS (OTHER THAN SURVIVING SPOUSES)

If taxable income is:	The tax is:
Not over $2,3000	No tax.
Over $2,300 but not over $3,400	14% of excess over $2,300.
Over $3,400 but not over $4,400	$54, plus 16% of excess over $3,400.
Over $4,400 but not over $6,500	$314, plus 18% of excess over $4,400.
Over $6,500 but not over $8,500	$692, plus 19% of excess over $6,500.
Over $8,500 but not over $10,800	$1,072, plus 21% of excess over $8,500.
Over $10,800 but not over $12,900	$1,555, plus 24% of excess over $10,800.
Over $12,900 but not over $15,000	$2,059, plus 26% of excess over $12,900.
Over $15,000 but not over $18,200	$2,605, plus 30% of excess over $15,000.
Over $18,200 but not over $23,500	$3,565, plus 34% of excess over $18,200.
Over $23,500 but not over $28,800	$5,367, plus 39% of excess over $23,500.
Over $28,800 but not over $34,100	$7,434, plus 44% of excess over $28,800.
Over $34,100 but not over $41,500	$9,766, plus 49% of excess over $34,100.
Over $41,500 but not over $55,300	$13,392, plus 55% of excess over $41,500.
Over $55,300 but not over $81,800	$20,982, plus 63% of excess over $55,300.
Over $81,800 but not over $108,300	$37,677, plus 68% of excess over $81,800.
Over $108,300	$55,697, plus 70% of excess over $108,300.

NOTES

NOTES

NOTES

NOTES

NOTES

NOTES

NOTES

NOTES